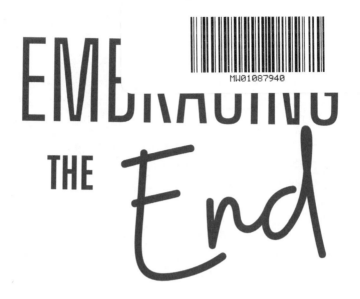

EMBRACING THE End

Discovering
peace
and purpose
at the end of life.

DEANNA COTTEN

Published by:
Wendy Melrose, Soel Love Books, LLC, www.soellovebooks.com
In The Zone, www.inthezone.live

Cover Design: Sarah Sechler, sjsechler11design@gmail.com

ISBN Paperback: 978-1-963294-02-6
ISBN Hardback: 978-1-963294-03-3
ISBN Ebook: 978-1-963294-04-0

Printed in the United States of America

For permissions or inquiries, please contact:
Wendy Melrose at www.inthezone.live

Scripture References:
Scripture taken from the New King James Version®. Copyright © 1982 by Thomas Nelson. Used by permission. All rights reserved.
Scripture quotations taken from The Holy Bible, New International Version® (NIV®). Copyright © 1973, 1978, 1984, 2011 by Biblica, Inc.® Used by permission. All rights reserved worldwide

Thank you for supporting Deanna's legacy and helping to share her story of resilience and hope.

Table of Contents

Bucket List

"I had a bucket list of things I wanted to accomplish before I passed. First of all I promised to never lose my sense of humor. I created a whole bucket list of things I wanted to accomplish before I died.

- Diamond Art project
- Buy my own urn
- Write my own obituary
- Arm sleeves tattooed
- Watched the end of Season 6 of the series "Virgin River", it left me hanging, so now I need to see Season 7?!
- Finish this Book

This book was the most important. Looks like I did it all before the "deadline", 'Season 7' looks like you are too far out, I will have a better view from Heaven.

– Deanna

Foreword

I t is always deeply profound to meet someone at the end of their life. Even more so when I am meeting them *because* they're dying.

As a palliative care chaplain and host of a podcast in which I interview people with terminal diagnoses, I meet several people each and every week who are coming to the end of their lives. Fortunately for me and, I think, for so many others, Deanna is one of those people I'm privileged to have met, not long after she received her terminal diagnosis of ALS.

A former coworker recommended her as a potential guest for the podcast. Finding the right fit has always been something of a conundrum. It takes a special person to be living with a terminal illness, accepting mortality, willing to discuss with a stranger, and willing for a bunch of other strangers to listen in on that conversation.

As I began watching Deanna discuss her diagnosis on social media, what struck me most was her honesty. She went right at the issues she was talking about and, though always kind, did not mince words about the reality of her own mortality. When I sent her a message to ask about her interest in being a guest, she was immediately excited—sharing her story was her mission.

My first conversation with Deanna was a little over two hours long. She had just started hospice care and she talked openly and frankly with me about her decision to forgo some of the life-saving interventions commonly used with people who share her diagnosis. I immediately knew that this episode of the podcast would be wonderful, and that a friendship was quickly forming.

I have spent time with thousands of people who are living with terminal illness. The perspective that Deanna shares and the lens of faith through which she sees her story is truly unique. But perhaps most refreshing is the stripped-down honesty with which Deanna shares her struggles. Never with a sense of shame. Rather, Deanna is eager to include her struggles, and indeed her failures, as an acceptable, even a celebrated part of her story.

In that first conversation, we eventually ended up in a celebratory exclamation as we agreed that only people who have struggled can truly know what Saint Paul meant when he wrote in Philippians 4:13, "I can do all things through Christ who strengthens me."

The Apostle is not talking there about being a great success, winning, or accomplishing some great achievement. He's talking about finding peace and contentment regardless of the life situations that he found himself in. Indeed, Deanna's story is about many things. One of the most impactful is her ability to struggle through difficult times and find peace within herself through faith. Her acceptance of her mortality, her sincere positivity, her joy, and her friendship have been inspiring to me, and I believe they will be to you as well.

There is no way around the fact that, as I write this, Deanna is nearing the end of her life. And to honor a request she shared on the podcast, I will not plead for more days for her. Instead, I will remember her story and continue to learn what it means to accept what comes, learn from difficulties, and to find the joy, peace, and contentment available in each moment—in Deanna's words, "to truly live."

I hope and believe you will too.

Cody Hufstedler
Host, *Dying To Tell You*

You can visit his website to the podcast "Dying to Tell You" here:

Scan to go to https://dttypodcast .com/

The Great Period Panic: A False Alarm for the Ages

My first question when I get to Heaven will be—'Lord, why did You let Aunt Flow keep visiting when I can't even stand to greet her?!'

There is nothing in my body that works correctly—except for one damn thing that shows up every single month, on time, like a bill collector that refuses to be ignored. And when it comes, oh boy, it comes. There's one day in particular when the floodgates open, and I'm just out here bleeding through my pants like some kind of crime scene waiting to happen. Oh, and sleep? Gone. Poof.

So, of course, on my heaviest day, I had physical therapy. Because why not? Just to be safe, I doubled up on pads, reinforced the perimeter like I was preparing for battle, and thought I was all set. Before I left for PT, I even did a fresh swap—because I am a responsible adult who takes precautions.

Fast forward to my session: My therapist started stretching my arm, and I was already feeling the strain, but then—BAM. A gush. And not the good kind. The kind that makes your stomach drop and your soul leave your body. To make matters worse, I was wrapped in white towels for warmth. WHITE. TOWELS.
I immediately panicked. "Oh sh!t."

I stopped everything. "Listen," I said, "I have a confession. I'm pretty sure I just bled through my pants."

The two therapists—absolute professionals—remained calm. "Do you want some shorts? Or should we take you to the bathroom?"
At this point, I was beyond mortified. I was ready to fake my own death and start a new life in another state. But they were cool about it, which was nice.

The Great Period Panic: Cont'...

Then came the moment of truth. We lifted my leg to assess the damage, and... nothing.
Nothing!

I had made this entire dramatic scene for absolutely no reason. I nearly shut down a whole PT session over a false alarm. To this day, we still laugh about it. And now, every time I walk in, they ask, "Do you have an extra pad on?"

Every. Damn. Time.

– Deanna

Life in the Fast Lane, Part 1

L ife slowed down to a crawl—before both near-death experiences forced me to reexamine everything—I had been speeding through life without a second thought. Like so many, I wore my busyness as a badge of honor. Productivity became my purpose, and if I wasn't moving forward, I felt like I was failing.

Because of my personality style and drive, my coach was always telling me, "You are really good at being a human doing—you need to learn how to be a human being." I laughed it off at the time, but deep down, I knew there was truth in those words. I was so focused on accomplishing, achieving, and pushing forward that I had forgotten how to just *be*.

I was an entrepreneur, a mom, a wife, a friend—the kind of person who tried to do it all. My days started early, ended late, and were packed with tasks and to-do lists that never seemed to get any shorter. I thought the grind was worth it, that all the sacrifices I was making would pay off in the end. But the truth is, I was neglecting the things that mattered most—my mental health which was affecting sense of peace preventing me from becoming my best self. At times, I even found myself daydreaming about usual morning rhythm. Then, out of nowhere, a car pulled into our path. I hit the brakes, but it was too late. We collided.

The impact was violent and immediate. Time slowed as I looked over at Laura, old enough to know better—she wasn't wearing her seatbelt. I had reminded her so many times, but like any teenager, she thought it was no big deal. Now, I watched helplessly as her body was thrown forward, her head hitting the windshield with a force that made my stomach lurch.

I will never forget yelling at her over and over again, "Why aren't you wearing a seatbelt?" as if I could change anything in that moment. I was mad at myself for not knowing she wasn't buckled. I was thankful she appeared okay, but angry that there was even a possibility she might not have been.

When I was a kid, my mom would slam on the brakes, and her arm would instinctively fly out to shield me from the dashboard. I do the same with my own kids. It's a reflex—part of the universal "mom code" to protect our children at all costs. But in this moment, I realized just how powerless I was. No amount of instinct or effort could have stopped the impact. I couldn't control this the way I so desperately wanted to.

When the car finally came to a stop, the silence was deafening. My youngest, sitting in the back, was crying—shaken but unharmed—more worried about the popcorn she had been eating for breakfast, now scattered all over the floor. Laura sat in stunned silence, conscious with tears, and fear filled the space between us.

I reached out, trembling, trying to assess the damage. Laura noticed I hadn't put a lid on my protein shake—the cup had flown out of the holder, and the shake had splattered across the dash, painting it with strawberry-banana chaos. She looked at me and said, 'Next time, put a lid on your shake.' In that moment, I knew we were okay. But I also knew that nothing would ever be the same. We were alive.

In the days and weeks after the accident, I replayed it over and over in my mind. Why hadn't I double-checked her seatbelt? Why didn't I leave earlier or take a different route? The "what ifs" haunted me.

Although the guilt was suffocating, I found myself moving into fight mode. I was pushing forward with everything in me, determined to do what needed to be done for Laura's recovery. At the same time, I was in a sort of flight mode—mentally running from the deeper wounds God was asking me to confront. This season was a constant tug-of-war between empowering myself to move forward and ignoring the weight of the past traumas I was carrying.

Months later we discovered Laura suffered a traumatic brain injury and permanent hearing loss. She would never hear the world the same way again, and I couldn't stop blaming myself.

The months that followed were a whirlwind of doctor's appointments, therapy sessions, and learning to navigate a new normal. Laura had to adjust to life with hearing aids, a process that came with its own challenges. School became increasingly difficult for her. She had already struggled with learning disabilities before the accident, but now those struggles were compounded.

As parents, we were becoming increasingly concerned because her confidence was suffering, and we did not want her to think she was a failure. So, we encouraged her to research unschooling. Eventually, she decided to drop out of the public school system, giving herself a better opportunity to learn in a way that would serve her new disability and boost her confidence.

Through it all, Laura's resilience began to shine. She didn't let her hearing loss define her or drag her down. Instead, she turned her challenge into an opportunity to make a difference. She started learning sign language and performed the Star-Spangled Banner at a football game her new language. Watching her on that field, I saw ashes turning into beauty.

This moment reminded me of all the times I questioned whether my kids truly heard the lessons I'd tried to instill in them. When they were little, I'd pour into them, wondering if anything I said or did would stick. Moments like this showed me that those seeds had taken root. I had taught my kids to see life's challenges as opportunities to rise up and help others, and here was Laura, living out that truth.

Her decision to use her experience to help others humbled me. She wasn't bitter or angry with anyone. Laura saw her hearing loss as an opportunity to grow, to learn, and to inspire others, especially teenagers to wear their seatbelt. Watching her strength gave me strength. It reminded me that God was writing her story just as He was writing mine. My role wasn't to control every detail; it was to teach, guide, and trust Him to direct her path.

"A man's heart plans his way, but the Lord directs his steps."
Proverbs 16:9 (NKJV)

One of the hardest lessons I've learned in life is that unhealed past traumas take an incredible toll on your life journey. No amount of guilt or sleepless nights spent replaying this accident could change what happened. I had to place the burden at the foot of the Cross for Him to carry it for me. That wasn't an easy process. I was angry—angry at myself, at the driver who caused the accident, and even at God. But slowly, through prayer and reflection, I began to see that holding onto that anger wasn't serving me or Laura. I had to surrender it to God, trusting that He would bring healing in His time and way.

Looking back now, I can see how this moment, as painful as it was, became a catalyst for growth—not just for Laura, but for me. This accident forced me to reevaluate what truly matters and to lean on God in ways I never had before. This was the beginning of me realizing that resilience isn't about avoiding pain; it's about finding purpose in the midst of it.

Laura's strength became my strength. Through her unexpected hearing loss, she was living out the lessons I had worked so hard to teach her. She reminded me that even in the most broken moments, there is potential for something beautiful. That accident may have changed everything, but it didn't define us. It refined us, revealing a depth of faith and resilience I didn't know we had, and would soon need more than ever before. God is good at preparing our hearts and minds for what we do not even know is coming.

But what if the greatest crash in your life isn't the kind that bends metal and shatters glass?
What if the real wreckage is the moment you realize you have to choose—fight or flight?

I chose to fight. And in fighting, I started wearing too many hats. If there were ever a badge for doing it all, I would've worn it proudly.

grown that season of life. My mission had always been about serving others. I wanted to use my gifts, talents, and strengths for God's glory. At my core, I longed to be a missionary in my own way, meeting needs wherever I found them. Somewhere along the way, I forgot how to simply be. My own business coach reminded me that I had become a 'human doing' instead of a 'human being.' That craving to win at life, to keep succeeding, was a very real thing. When something went wrong, I was always that "pick yourself up and keep on going" kind of gal.

In 2018, life threw another curveball when my oldest daughter, Ashley, became critically ill. At just 15, she spent weeks at Children's of Wisconsin and was discharged with a feeding tube and life-altering diagnoses: Chiari Malformation, POTS, and Ehlers-Danlos Syndrome. But just like her mom, she kept going. I watched her return to school and coach her Sinissippi Pom Squad as if nothing had happened.

Meanwhile, I was juggling a commercial cleaning business, managing employees, and surviving on a diet of a triangle pink-sprinkled donuts, and 32-ounce Pepsi from QT. On top of that, I was driving Ashley to two to four doctor's appointments in Milwaukee—45 minutes away—every week. Sleep became an afterthought, and exhaustion was my constant companion. But I pushed through because the bills didn't care, and the weight of responsibility felt too heavy to set down.

But that season came at a cost. I was dropping balls and making mistakes I couldn't afford. I had no choice—I had to reduce my client load by 75% because I had to choose between Ashley's care and maintaining the business. Our savings account was drained, and eventually, the stress caught up with me. We were forced to downsize from the beautiful Victorian home we had been renting (and considering buying) and move into a more affordable place under circumstances that left my heart shattered.

It was then that I learned a hard truth—not everyone who offers to help truly has your best interests at heart. The betrayal of losing friends and trust in others cut deeply, leaving wounds I carried for years. However, I have since developed clear boundaries to ensure we never end up in that position again. The Lord was nudging me to face the triggers tied to my traumas.

Looking back, I wish I had prioritized my mental health during those times. I thought I could repair and fix things on my own, but I didn't have the coping skills and time to navigate life's emergencies or the tools to face financial trauma head-on. Instead, I shoved the hardships into the background, convincing myself that resilience was just a mindset I could will myself into. I worked hard to provide for my family, to create opportunities for them, and to show them that my sacrifices were for their good. And while we enjoyed family vacations, retreats, and shared moments of connection, there was always a part of me that struggled to turn off the performer and just be present.

This balancing act wasn't manageable, and I knew it. My routines were consistent—morning prayers, evening reflections, strategic planning on par, goal-setting—but they became so rigid that I began to expect things to go wrong again. I thought I was resilient, but I would later learn the truth:

"Resilience is not a mindset. It is learned through patience, wisdom, and experience in the face of adversity." – Deanna Cotten

The relentless pace of life began to take its toll, not just on my body, but on my mind and soul. I wasn't neglecting my relationships—I had worked hard to prioritize time with my family and friends—but I struggled to let go of the need to always be "on" in performance mode. What I didn't realize was that I was entering a season where I could no longer hide from the life I was merely surviving. It wasn't until I was forced to stop that I saw the truth—I wasn't really living; I was just getting by. But God, in His infinite wisdom, was preparing me for what was to come. Each chapter of my life had been so difficult, and the cracks along with their trauma triggers were beginning to show.

This chapter of my life is a difficult one to revisit, but it's also necessary. It's where the cracks began to show—where I started to recognize the limits of my physical strength and the cost of pushing too hard for too long.

I was no stranger to a life filled with symptoms. Chronic illnesses like migraines, neuropathy, Hashimoto's, iron deficiency, and celiac disease had taught me to adapt quickly to each new "normal." So, when I first noticed weakness in my hands and pain that made writing scripture in my journal nearly impossible, I didn't ignore it. I assumed the symptoms were work-related, caused by long hours at my desk. I sought solutions—working with a physical therapist, adjusting my computer setup, chair, and work habits. I wasn't dismissive, but I also didn't push hard enough for answers.

I followed up with doctors, completed every test and scan, and tried their recommendations, but nothing worked. This was the prologue to a story of true resilience—one not about grinding through the pain, but about learning to heal, let go, and trust God in new and deeper ways.

I thought I was doing everything right—managing it all, keeping everything together, proving my strength by pushing through. But in reality, I was justifying my handwriting to my clients convincing them that I could read what I was writing. I was cancelling appointments with clients and often times not telling my employees that I was attending appointments that were life or death. I was starting to use a cane, I was sacrificing the very things that made life meaningful.

Have you ever stopped to ask yourself if the way you're living aligns with the life you actually want? Are you constantly doing, chasing the next goal, carrying the weight of responsibilities, without stopping to ask if it's costing you something greater?

The truth is, we can't keep running on empty without consequences. Eventually, something gives—our health, our relationships, our sense of purpose. And sometimes, we don't notice what we've lost until we look back and wonder how we missed it.

That's what happened to me. I was so focused on keeping up that I didn't realize what I was neglecting. The challenges and circumstances in life have a way of making you stop and take inventory—whether you're ready or not.

Before we can start living life on purpose, we have to face what we've been neglecting and then do something about it.

Chapter 3

NEGLECTING WHAT TRULY MATTERS

Life has a way of rushing past when you're busy chasing it. For years, I thought I was doing what mattered most: building a successful business as a coach and consultant, setting my family up for a brighter future, and proving to myself and the world that I could handle anything thrown my way. My family was my motivation—I wanted to give them opportunities, plan meaningful trips, and create memories they would cherish forever. I worked hard to show them that my sacrifices weren't just for my clients but for them too. They may not have always seen it that way, but my true heart was for them to be blessed by my success.

But out of that desire to provide and to gain their blessing for my busyness, I pushed myself harder and harder. My days were a blur of to-do lists and endless deadlines. There was always one more project, one more client, one more fire to put out. "I'll make it up to them later," I'd think as I stayed late at the office or took on another responsibility. But "later" kept slipping further away.

Looking back, I realize I wasn't just working for them—I was also distracting myself. Slowing down would've meant confronting things I wasn't ready to face. I thought I had already overcome my past traumas, but deep down, they were stirring in me. God had been tugging at my heartstrings to pursue trauma therapy, but I ignored His call. I told myself that life was fine, that I had already done enough healing. And besides, I didn't want one more thing added to my busy schedule. I was avoiding therapy, thinking I could fix it on my own. I didn't see that avoiding those wounds was preventing me from experiencing true forgiveness, restoration, and the abundance of life God wanted for me.

It wasn't that I was neglecting my relationships. In fact, I was planning purposeful family vacations and one-on-one trips with my kids. I wanted to invest in them, and I thought I was doing it well. But what I didn't see was that I was avoiding difficult places of unhealed pain. I mistook the resurfacing of those traumas as the enemy trying to steal my joy, rather than God calling me to heal. By avoiding those difficult places, I was also avoiding the deeper breakthrough God had in store for me.

The cost of chasing busy wasn't just physical—it was spiritual and emotional. I was missing out on experiencing life through the lens of healing and forgiveness. The energy I poured into working hard for my family could have been spent facing those triggers head-on, pursuing restoration and stepping into the new heights God was preparing for me.

I'll never forget the night my daughter had a school play. She had practiced her lines for weeks, excitedly telling me about her role and how she couldn't wait for me to see her on stage. But that evening, a work emergency came up, and I stayed home, glued to my laptop. "It's just one night," I told myself. "She'll understand."

As she left for the performance, I saw her look back at me from the doorway, her smile a little dimmer than usual. That image stayed with me. I wasn't just missing moments—I was missing her, her gifts and talents. The next morning, she told me about the play and showed me her costume, but something had shifted. I realized I couldn't keep letting these moments pass me by.

But my greatest regrets didn't come from missing those performances or conversations—they came from purposeful avoidance. I thought I was protecting my peace, but in reality, I was building walls that kept me from healing. Those walls were also keeping me from fully living.

The change didn't happen overnight. It started with small realizations—a family photo that reminded me of how we used to laugh together, a conversation with a friend about her father's terminal illness that reminded me how precious time is. Piece by piece, I began to see the truth: life isn't about how much you accomplish; it's about who you share it with, how fully you embrace the moments you're given, and the impact you make along the way.

One evening, I finally put down my phone and asked my daughter about her day. She looked surprised—maybe even a little suspicious—but as we talked, I saw her face light up in a way I hadn't seen in years. Slowly, I started carving out more intentional time for my family. I started choosing connection over tasks, presence over productivity. When I was driving the kids around to their activities, we became intentional with talking about their day to day lives. I also started leaning into God's call to heal, realizing that the only way to move forward was to stop avoiding my past.

This chapter is my reminder to you—and to myself—that the grind isn't worth it if it costs you the people you love or the healing God has for you.

Success isn't measured by the accolades you earn or the wealth you accumulate. It's measured by the love you give, the connections you nurture, and the peace you find in God's presence.

Life is short for all of us, I encourage you to pause. Look around at your life. Are you fully present with the people who matter most? Are you pushing forward so hard that you're missing the moments that make life meaningful? Are there unhealed wounds holding you back from the life God wants for you?

Don't wait until regret whispers in the silence. Sometimes, life doesn't tap you on the shoulder—it shakes you awake. It forces you to stop, to see clearly, and to realize what you've been neglecting.

For me, that moment came suddenly, violently—without warning. What if the wake-up call you've been avoiding comes in a way you never expected?

Before you turn the page, I want you to ask yourself: What would it take for you to start living life on purpose right now, before you have no choice?

Psalm 90:12 (NIV) *"Teach us to number our days, that we may gain a heart of wisdom."*

The Crash of the Soul, Part 2

There's a unique kind of pain that comes with the unraveling of who you thought you were. It doesn't happen all at once—it's a slow, agonizing process that chips away at your identity, your dreams, and your sense of control. Outsiders often see major events in our lives as something you just walk into and back out of like it is a linear process. However, this season of my life "The Crash of the Soul" was exactly the opposite, a rollercoaster ride. Everything I thought I knew about myself, about God, and about life came crashing down.

It wasn't just the unraveling of who I thought I was—it was the unearthing of what I thought I had already healed from. Past traumas I had tucked away, thinking they were dealt with, began bubbling to the surface. It became painfully clear how much I had bottled up to "deal with later," and now, later had arrived.

Previously, I shared what it was like to live in the fast lane, juggling responsibilities and chasing success, all while unknowingly setting the stage for a breaking point. But this part of the story isn't about the busy life I lived. It's about the moment when the brakes slammed hard, forcing me to confront the weight of it all.

My faith wavered, my anger burned hot, and my fear threatened to consume me. It is where I learn what it truly means to wrestle with God. It's where I began to see that resilience isn't just about holding on—it's about learning to let go. Letting go of guilt, letting go of control, and letting go of the belief that I could navigate life's storms on my own.

I used to think resilience was about sheer willpower, about muscling through hard times. But I've learned something far deeper: *"Resilience is not a mindset. It is learned through patience, wisdom, and experience in the face of adversity."* These words have become a mantra for me—a reminder that resilience isn't about perfection or strength but about growth and surrender in the hardest moments.

I like to think of resilience as a mountain standing before me. Climbing uphill is the battle—the test of resilience. You don't stand at the base of the mountain and declare, *"I am resilient."* Resilience is something you discover *as* you climb, step by step, gaining strength and confidence along the way.

But we have a choice. We can stand at the base, refusing to climb, resisting the struggle altogether. And when we do, we miss out. We miss out on the healing, the growth, and the power that come from reaching the other side. It remains unknown—what we *could* have gained, who we *could* have become.

Then, when you finally reach the top and begin the journey back down, you do so knowing—you *are* resilient. The lessons I've learned were forged in fire, tested in struggle. Without resistance, there would be no strength to gain. It is in the climb that resilience is built.

Trauma and loss broke me open, stripping away every illusion of control I held so tightly. I battled my beliefs and faith like never before. But in the breaking, there was also room for something new: a faith that wasn't polished but real. A hope that wasn't unshaken but alive. And a resilience that wasn't about my own strength but about God's ability to carry me when I couldn't carry myself.

I had avoided confronting the parts of myself I had avoided for so long. There was a divine purpose in facing the grief, anger, and pain I had tried to ignore—one that became clear in the midst of the crash. A purpose that would not only bring healing, hope, and strength to me but also to the relationships I cherished and the life I was determined to live fully.

I lived a life in overdrive to one that began to slow down, not by choice but by necessity. It's the story of how God met me in the wreckage of my soul and began to piece it back together. Not perfectly, but beautifully, with a purpose I am still learning to understand.

If you're walking through your own crash—whether it's of the soul, the heart, or the spirit—know this: even in the wreckage, there is hope. Even in the fire, something new can rise. And even in the moments when it feels like all is lost, God is not finished. He is still writing your story, just as He is still writing mine.

Chapter 4

THE SILENCE AFTER THE STORM

When the dust settles after a storm, you expect relief. You hope for clarity or, at the very least, a moment to breathe. But what they don't tell you is how loud silence can be. After my near-death experience on the icy roads of Wyoming, I wasn't met with peace or resolution. Instead, I was left with questions, fears, and an unsettling quiet that seemed to echo inside me.

I didn't know it at the time, but this silence was its own kind of storm. As an open book online, you could trace back to January 2023 on how quiet I was in the fight.

In the days after the accident, I couldn't shake the thought that I was supposed to be gone. I replayed those three seconds over and over—the semi barreling toward me, the headlights stared at me in the face I thought it was daytime, the steering wheel clenched in my hands, and the inexplicable gap of air, or angel wings, that saved my life. Everyone called it a miracle, and I knew in my heart it was. But instead of gratitude, I felt something darker: rejection.

For months, I struggled to reconcile my purpose here on earth with the perfect healing I imagined in heaven. I felt rejected at heaven's gates, as though God had told me I wasn't good enough to enter. Although I understood my faith and knew my salvation wasn't earned, I couldn't see past the fact that I was so close. I was right there. I saw the light.

My children, my husband, my dreams, and my goals were enough to live for, and I could say that out loud. But the emotional and mental pain of staying and working toward healing felt unbearable. Every day I woke up from what could have been, and heaven still seemed more appealing. My loved ones, my friends, my gifts, and my talents—I convinced myself they would all be fine without me. I struggled to find a way forward, even as the world around me moved on.

Everyday, for nearly three years, I drove the same path to drop my kids off at school and get to my office. We took the same exit off the interstate at 7:45 a.m., five days a week. And every morning, without fail, we saw Miss Lorraine. She was a homeless woman who panhandled at the same intersection, rain or shine.

Many people probably saw her as just another person begging for change, but I saw something more. She was faithful. Reliable. She showed up every day, no matter how bad the weather was. While we never gave her money, except at Christmas, we always rolled the window down and had a short conversation with her. Her face would light up and she always seemed to enjoy the short conversation until the light turned green.

After my accident, those conversations took on a new meaning. They became an anchor in the storm of my mind, a reminder that I still had purpose on this side of heaven. Miss Lorraine didn't know I had almost died. She had no idea I was struggling to get behind the wheel every day.

Driving just to school and work felt like climbing a mountain, day after day. But her smile and the brief exchange of kind words at that stoplight became a lifeline for me.

It wasn't about the act of giving or what I could do for her; it was about connection. Seeing her face light up because we took the time to ask how she was doing reminded me that God's mission for me wasn't about grand gestures or monumental achievements. It was about the simple, faithful acts of love and kindness that ripple through the lives of others.

The silence after the accident wasn't just external—it was internal too. For the first time in my life, I couldn't hear God's voice. I prayed. I begged. But the heavens felt closed to me. God had always been my refuge, my place of comfort, but now He felt distant. And that distance terrified me.

I thought about giving up, about closing the door to Him altogether. But something inside me wouldn't let go. So I did the only thing I could: I sat in the silence. I stopped trying to fill it with noise or distractions. I stopped demanding answers. I let myself feel the ache of uncertainty.

Slowly, something began to shift. It started with small moments. Watching my kids laugh at the dinner table. Holding my husband's hand during a movie. Catching a sunset that painted the sky in colors so vivid it took my breath away. These were the things I had almost missed. These were the things that reminded me why I was still here.

Miss Lorraine was part of that shift too. Her steadfast presence at that stoplight became a symbol of God's faithfulness. She reminded me that it wasn't up to me to decide when I was ready for heaven. That was God's call, and until then, my mission here wasn't finished.

The silence became less about what I didn't know and more about what I did. I didn't know why I had been spared, but I knew my life wasn't over yet. I didn't know what the future held, but I knew I had today. And maybe that was enough.

Looking back now, I see those weeks of silence as a gift. They forced me to slow down, to sit with my fears, and to wrestle with the questions I'd been too busy to ask. They showed me that faith isn't about having all the answers—it's about trusting in the unknown. It's about believing that even in the quiet, God is still there.

That silence after the storm wasn't the end of my journey. It was the beginning of a deeper one. One where I would learn to embrace uncertainty, to find strength in vulnerability, and to live with a renewed sense of purpose. It wasn't an easy lesson, and it didn't happen overnight. But it was a turning point—a quiet, sacred moment where I began to rebuild my soul and reconnect by hearing from God again. Just me and Him.

When the storm passes, when the silence settles in, what do you do next?

Maybe you've faced a moment like that—the kind that shakes you to your core, leaving you questioning everything. Maybe you've wrestled with the silence, with the weight of the unknown, with the feeling that life as you knew it would never be the same.

But what if the silence isn't just emptiness? What if, in that quiet, there's an invitation—to sit with the questions, to listen for the whispers of truth, to stop running from the things we've buried for too long?

I didn't realize it then, but God was preparing me for the hardest chapter of my life. The silence wasn't rejection—it was preparation.

And maybe, just maybe, your silence is preparing you too.

Chapter 5

Anger at God

When the doctor said, "I'm 95% sure this is ALS," I sat there, confused because I didn't know what ALS was even though I knew others who had it. The doctor asked, "Deanna, do you want me to shoot straight with you?" I said, yes. He continued, "ALS, also known as Lou Gehrig Disease, is a neurodegenerative disease that is 100% fatal, with a 2-5 year life expectancy from the onset of symptoms." *(People have subtle symptoms for a long time and it goes undiagnosed because there is no exact test. It is diagnosed by process of elimination of mimicking diseases. Once they are all ruled out, the EMG becomes the final test to confirm)* I already knew in my gut what the tests would confirm, but I repeated in my mind him saying Ninety-five percent. I wanted to cling to that 5% as if it were my lifeline. That sliver of hope was all I had in the moment, and I couldn't bring myself to let go.

I've always been a woman of faith. I was in church my entire life, but I didn't come to have a relationship with the Lord until I was 25 years old. Since then I have been steeped in scripture, prayer that felt personal and real. Yet, when life's storms came crashing over me—one after another—I found myself wrestling with emotions I never expected to feel toward my Creator: anger and rejection, AGAIN!! Not fleeting frustration, but deep, consuming emotions that shook the foundations of my belief.

I walked to my car, the weight of those words pressing down on me until I could hardly breathe. I gripped the steering wheel, replaying the moment over and over, feeling utterly blindsided. I screamed, "WHY ME, GOD!?!? Why now? Hadn't I been through enough?" I wasn't pleading for healing or even for more time—I was just begging for an answer. I needed to know why He would allow this to happen. Wasn't I faithful enough? Strong enough? Hadn't I done everything I was supposed to do? It felt like I had been cast out, left to navigate this impossible road alone.

The shock was paralyzing. It wasn't just anger or fear; it was a profound sense of being thrown off course. I had experienced so much healing in my life—emotional, relational, and spiritual. I had found purpose, joy, and hope. Now, it felt like the rug had been pulled out from under me.

I couldn't bring myself to share the diagnosis with anyone—not my husband, not my best friend, not even my prayer warriors. My husband holds grudges and I didn't want to burden him with something that might turn out to be wrong. I couldn't imagine misleading those closest to me with the words, "Deanna, you're dying," only to discover the doctor had been wrong.

Instead, I turned my face to the wall, just me and God, no outside influence, and I prayed. In that intimate, solitary moment, it was just me and God. My prayers began as desperate pleas: *Please, God, don't let it be ALS.* But soon, they shifted. As my prayers evolved, I stopped begging for it to be something else. Instead, I asked, *Lord, meet me here in this place.*

At times, I found myself pleading for anything else, then quickly catching myself. What if "anything else" turned out to be far worse? I asked for wisdom for the doctors, clarity for the road ahead, and strength to face whatever was coming. My prayers became less about changing my circumstances and more about hearing from God in the midst of them.

One day, in the quiet of those moments with God, He asked me a question that pierced straight through my heart: *"Do you still believe what you said you believed?"* Instantly, I knew what He meant. My testimony the entire year after the accident, was that I wasn't afraid to die. I needed a moment to process, to search my heart and revisit the memories of my brush with death.

I thought back to the icy Wyoming highway, where my car spun toward a semi-truck, just a year earlier, and I knew it was over. But instead of fear, I was filled with fury. I wasn't afraid to die—I was furious that I didn't get to say goodbye. Furious that something so mundane as black ice could rip me away from my family.

I wasn't afraid to die then, and I realized with a deep, unshakable certainty that I wasn't afraid to die now. This wasn't just a truth I spoke—it was a shift in my spirit. I felt a peace that surpassed all understanding. With confidence, I agreed with God: *"I am still not afraid to die."*

Then He said something that stopped me in my tracks: *"I have shown you favor."* At first, I didn't understand. Favor? How could this diagnosis be favor? But as I sat with His words, I began to see the truth. I had begged for more time—not just to live, but to prepare my family, to say goodbye, to leave them well. And this terminal diagnosis was God's way of answering that prayer.

Before I shared my diagnosis with anyone, God gave me the gift of clarity through the story of Hezekiah.

> *"Then Hezekiah turned his face toward the wall, and prayed to the LORD, and said, 'Remember now, O LORD, I pray, how I have walked before You in truth and with a loyal heart, and have done what is good in Your sight.' And Hezekiah wept bitterly."* (2 Kings 20:2-3)

Hezekiah, terminally ill, turned his face to the wall and pleaded with God for his life. God heard his prayer, saw his tears, and extended his life by 15 years. But those extra years came with challenges, and ultimately, Hezekiah's spiritual journey faltered.

The wisdom I gained from Hezekiah's story shaped how I approached my own terminal diagnosis before anyone else knew about it and before their opinions could try to shape my understanding of how God could work in this situation in my life. God had given me time—not endless, open-ended time, but precious, finite time to fulfill His purpose for my life. I found peace in surrendering my timeline to God. I didn't need to plead for healing. I needed to trust Him with the time I had left.

I AM HEALED! I AM HEALED! I AM HEALED!

I wept when I realized the truth: God hadn't abandoned me. He was answering my prayers, just not in the way I expected. I was sad, I was mad, I was angry, but also blessed that he answered my prayers. That realization didn't erase the weight of my diagnosis or the days when the burden feels too heavy to carry. But it gave me a foundation of peace.

Now, when I pray, it's not for more time or even for healing. It's for the strength to make the most of every moment. It's for my family to see resilience, not in my ability to deny pain but in my trust that God is carrying me through it. I pray my children will remember not my disease, but the love and faith that defined my life.

The following scripture has been a constant source of understanding and now, comfort. . .

"Trust in the Lord with all your heart, And lean not on your own understanding; In all your ways acknowledge Him, And He shall direct your paths." (Proverbs 3: 5-6)

God met me in that place with a peace and comfort that surpasses all understanding. He didn't scold me for my questions or doubts. He met me with grace, reminding me that His plans are good, even when they hurt.

Anger at God is no longer something I shy away from. It's part of the journey, a necessary step in wrestling with the hard questions to find the peace that lies on the other side. Every time I bring my raw, honest heart to Him, He is faithful to meet me there. And for that, I am grateful.

This chapter of my life has taught me that faith isn't about having all the answers. It's about trusting the One who does. I'm not afraid to die, but while I live, I will use this time to love deeply, live fully, and glorify God in every moment. I AM HEALED—not in body, but in spirit. And that, to me, is the greatest healing of all.

What if the very thing you fear the most—the loss, the hardship, the unexpected turn—was actually an invitation? Not to despair, but to live with greater purpose. Not to shrink back, but to lean in.

We don't always get advance notice when life changes forever. Sometimes, it comes in a crash. Other times, in a quiet diagnosis. But every moment—every breath—we are given is an opportunity.

So, I ask you: Are you truly living? Are you making the most of the time you have, or are you waiting for a wake-up call?

Because the truth is, we don't have to face death to start embracing life.

Chapter 6

KNOCKING AT DEATH'S DOOR AGAIN

Facing death once changes you. Facing it twice? It transforms you. I never imagined I'd be brought to that edge again, staring mortality square in the face. The first time, it left me shaken and questioning. The second time? It taught me how to truly live.

Remember, the first brush came on a frigid January day in 2023, with Wyoming's unforgiving black ice beneath my tires. As my car spun out of control, I wasn't afraid of dying. What haunted me in those frozen seconds was the thought of leaving my family without saying goodbye. The ache of unfinished moments weighed heavier than the impending crash. By some divine intervention, the crash didn't happen. I was spared. Just like Hezekiah in 2 Kings 20:2-3, I pled for my life and God honored it.

Fast forward to 2024. This time, the blow didn't come on icy roads but in the sterile quiet of a doctor's office. ALS. The words landed like a hammer. There was no escape, no bargaining with this reality. As I walked out of that office, the weight of those three letters pressed down on me until I could hardly breathe. I gripped the steering wheel, replaying the moment over and over, feeling utterly blindsided.

Before I had told anyone about my diagnosis, I turned to prayer. During that time, the Lord showed me something extraordinary: He had already answered my prayer. I thought back to the moment on the icy road when I had begged for more time—not out of fear of death, but out of a deep need to prepare my family, to say goodbye the way I hadn't been able to in that near miss. The Lord whispered to my heart, "Deanna, I gave you what you asked for. This is your time to say goodbye."

That realization shifts everything. What the world might see as a curse, I begin to see as a gift. God has given me something precious: **TIME.** Time to make memories, to pour into my family, to create a legacy of love and faith. It is finite, yes, but it is enough.

The laughter of my children feels sweeter. My husband's hand in mine is an anchor. Conversations with friends take on a new depth. The journey isn't easy. There are moments of deep grief, days when the weight of what I am losing feels unbearable. The sky feels darker, the trees aren't beautiful enough, the grass isn't green enough, the flowers aren't colorful enough. The beauty of this world can no longer compare to how the Lord is preparing me for the beauty that Heaven holds.

Living with ALS teaches me to embrace life with a different kind of urgency. I no longer take moments for granted. Every experience is an opportunity to create a memory. I take more pictures and videos than ever before—not because I'm afraid of forgetting, but because I want to savor each moment as if it could be the last. Whether it's touching the sand, flying on a plane, or savoring a perfectly brewed cup of coffee, I treat each one as a gift. If I get to experience it again, it's an added blessing. If I don't, I know I didn't miss out.

These two near-death experiences reshape my perspective. I no longer see time as something to be filled but as something to be cherished. I've also learned to use every opportunity to reach others for Christ or serve them in ways I might have been too busy for in the past. What once felt like burdens now feel like blessings.

Looking back, I see how God has been faithful through it all. He takes what could have been my end and turns it into a beginning—a chance to live with intention and to leave a legacy of faith and love.

If there's one thing I've learned, it's that the best way to face death is to fully embrace life. It's about seeing every moment as a gift and every interaction as an opportunity to reflect God's love. These experiences don't weaken me. They strengthen me, building a resilience that comes not from avoiding pain but from trusting God to carry me through it.

I am not scared to die. And because of that, I am finally learning how to truly live.

What if resilience isn't something you build after the storm, but something you choose before it ever comes?

We don't have to wait for a diagnosis, a crisis, or a breaking point to start living your best life. We don't have to wait for life to strip everything away before we realize what truly matters. The truth is, resilience isn't just about surviving the hard things—it's about making the most of every moment before they come.

I do not have to be dying to live on purpose. And neither do you.

I've learned that resilience isn't about having all the answers or never feeling afraid. It's about showing up for your life, even when it's messy. It's about choosing to love deeply, embrace joy, and lean into faith before you're forced to. Because when the storms hit—and they will—you'll already know what you're standing on.

"Think of yourself as dead. You have lived your life. Now take what's left and live it properly."
Marcus Aurelius

My journey isn't about waiting for the perfect circumstances to live. It's about stepping into each day with intention, hope, and a willingness to keep going, even when the road ahead is uncertain.

What are you waiting for?

If you're holding back, waiting for the perfect time to start living fully, let this be your wake-up call. Because life isn't found in the waiting—it's found in the living.

Now, let's walk this next part together.

First Class Fiasco: Champagne Showers and Sleeper Pods

Normally, Oren and I would never be caught dead in first class—unless we were sneaking a peek while shuffling past to our rightful seats in the back of the plane. But this time, we had business/first class tickets gifted to us. GIFTED. That meant we belonged here... at least for these flights. And let me tell you, we soaked up every last bit of that luxury.

Between the priority boarding (sometimes) and the extra legroom (which Oren enjoyed on my behalf), we kept looking at each other like, Why don't we do this all the time? Then we remembered we were not, in fact, real first-class people. But we played the part.

Our grand adventure took us from Punta Cana to Washington, D.C., where we had a layover that would test our speed, endurance, and bladder control. Typically, wheelchairs get you straight to the front of the line. Not this time. We had 15 minutes before our next flight departed, and we were still stuck in customs. Oh, and I had to pee. BAD.

Oren, the ever-practical husband, looked me dead in the eyes and said, "We do not have time. You will have to hold it until the next flight."

Hold it?! HOLD IT?!

With no other option, Oren took off sprinting, pushing me in my wheelchair like he was competing in the Olympic bobsled finals. We zig-zagged through the airport, dodging confused travelers and rogue rolling suitcases. My bladder was protesting, my dignity was hanging on by a thread, and then—miracle of miracles—we reached the gate.

First Class Fiasco: con't...

There stood the pilot, casually leaning against the door like he had just been waiting for us. "There are my seats 1A and 1B. We're glad you made it."

OH, SO ARE WE, CAPTAIN.

We rolled onto the plane, breathless, sweaty, and half-panicked. The flight attendant took one look at us and, in the kind of voice usually reserved for toddlers after a meltdown, said, "Would you like a glass of champagne to calm your nerves?"

YES. YES, WE WOULD.

We settled into our sleeper pods, which immediately turned us into giddy children wanting to push every button and try every feature. What?! WE WERE LUCKY. This was our moment, and we were going to recline and bask in it.

As I held my glass of champagne, I reminded myself to keep a tight grip because my hands don't always do what they're supposed to do. And yet, in true Deanna fashion, I dropped the entire thing in my lap.
And just like that, I looked like I had peed my pants.

I tried to dry myself off with the fancy first-class blanket, but now I just smelled like champagne-soaked regret.

The plane was gearing up for takeoff, so I leaned over and casually asked the flight attendant, "Hey, can I keep this blanket?" He smirked, nodded, and later even helped me clean up, which, honestly, should be a first-class amenity for people like me.

First Class Fiasco: con't...

Eventually, nature demanded its due, and I had to waddle to the bathroom. As I passed the rest of the flight crew, I felt compelled to explain.

"This isn't pee—it's champagne!" I announced proudly, as if that somehow made it better.

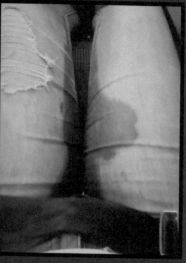

The attendants laughed their faces off and assured us that Oren and I were the coolest passengers they had ever met.

View of Deanna's pants after the Champagne spilled.

I grinned and said, "Well, we've never flown first class before, so we didn't know we needed to push the button eight times. We're not normally real first-class passengers."

And just like that, our accidental first-class experience became legendary.

-Deanna

The Resilience Blueprint, Part 3

Resilience isn't something you wake up one day and decide to have. It's not a switch you flip or a mantra you repeat until it sticks. It's something you forge in the fire of adversity, piece by painful piece. For me, resilience has been less about strength and more about surrender—letting go of what I can't control and leaning into what I can.

I cannot pretend I have it all figured out. It's about the tools and truths I've uncovered along the way: the moments in trauma counseling where I faced the raw weight of loss, the unexpected freedom that came from learning to be vulnerable, and the quiet strength I found in simply continuing forward. Resilience has been a process of rebuilding, not just enduring.

I'll share how I've learned to navigate the complexities of living with a terminal illness while still finding purpose and peace at the end of life. These aren't polished lessons from someone who has it all together; they're honest reflections from someone still living it out day by day. They're for anyone who's ever felt like they've been brought to the edge of themselves and wondered how to keep going.

This is the blueprint I've been sketching with shaky hands and a willing heart. It's not perfect, but it's real. And I hope it helps you find a little more courage, a little more hope, and a little more faith to face whatever storms come your way. Let's explore resilience together—not as a destination, but as a way of walking through the valleys with grace.

We all want to believe we'll be strong when life throws the unimaginable at us. But real resilience isn't built in the moment of crisis—it's formed in the small, unseen choices long before the storm ever comes.

We don't wake up one day with unshakable faith or the ability to endure whatever life brings. It's something we develop through trust, surrender, and sometimes, through the painful process of letting go of control.

This next chapter isn't just about resilience in theory—it's about resilience in practice. It's about the messy, real-life moments where faith is tested, where healing requires more than just prayer, and where strength doesn't always look like we expect.

How are you coping with the experience of receiving a diagnosis—whether for yourself or a loved one? Do you feel like you're constantly chasing medical miracles that drain your bank account? Do you find yourself trying to force healing? Do you long to surrender but struggle because your loved ones don't want you to?

I have been there and am here now. I can totally relate to all of this and wish I could hold your hand as you walk through life's hardest battles, with faith, wisdom, and the willingness to face the challenge in front of you and make the most of it.

Facing your death maybe the most difficult period of time in your life, but at the same time could become the most fulfilling.

Let's explore what it truly means to face life's toughest battles with faith, wisdom, and the strength to move forward.

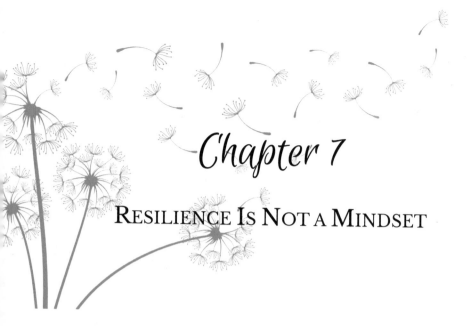

Chapter 7

RESILIENCE IS NOT A MINDSET

When people tell me I'm strong, I smile—not out of false modesty, but because they don't see the full picture. Strength is not what they think—it's not just stoic courage or unshakable faith. They don't see the whole picture. True strength is knowing to lean on God before the strength runs out, facing life's uncertainties with faith, and embracing each day with purpose, even when tomorrow is unclear.

The day I received my ALS diagnosis felt like a line was drawn in the sand. On one side, there was the life I had known—busy, productive, and full of plans for the future. On the other, a stark reality I couldn't escape. It wasn't resilience that carried me through those early moments; it was shock. But as the days passed, I realized resilience wasn't a single decision—it was a series of small, quiet choices to find the strength I needed in that very moment to keep moving forward.

Resilience has taken on a whole new meaning for me. I used to think it was about sheer determination—pushing through challenges, staying strong in the face of adversity. But living with ALS has taught me that resilience is less about pushing and more about surrendering. It's about acknowledging what I can't control while still making the most of what I can.

One of the biggest lessons I've learned is that resilience often looks like rest. On days when my body feels like it's giving up, I've learned to listen. With the help of my hospice nurses, I have learned not to sacrifice my sleep and rest. I intentionally give myself permission to slow down, say no, and allow others to step in. It's not weakness—it's wisdom. God has shown me that rest is not the opposite of resilience; it's part of it.

Another surprising lesson is how resilience reveals itself in community. There's a beautiful strength in allowing others to hold you up when you can't stand on your own. Whether it's my family stepping in with practical help, a friend showing up with coffee and conversation, or strangers offering prayer and encouragement, I've seen the hands and feet of God through people around me.

Living with ALS has made me see life differently. I've started to find joy in the little things—a favorite song playing on the radio in the car with my kids, the laughter of my kids, the warmth of a hug. Despite the fatigue I've also stopped putting off moments that matter. I take the trip. I make the phone call. I capture the memories, post them on social media. My family thinks my nose is always in my phone, but in reality, I'm over here capturing every memory I can—not because I'm afraid of running out of time, but because I know how precious each moment is. What they don't know is that shortly after my passing, they will discover over 15,000 memories I've captured—ready to be cherished forever and downloaded to their own phones.

Resilience also means staying present, even when it would be easier to check out. I've learned to engage with my family, to have difficult conversations, and to laugh even when life feels heavy. Resilience doesn't mean pretending everything is okay; it means choosing to live fully in spite of what isn't.

The truth is, I don't feel strong most days. But I've learned that strength isn't about feeling invincible—it's about trusting God when I feel anything but. It's not worth sacrificing relationships, and I don't want to lose a single moment, even when I'm exhausted. Strength is about finding hope in His promises, peace in His presence, and joy in His blessings. Resilience isn't something I've achieved on my own; it has been shaped in me by a faithful God who meets me in every moment.

There's a peace I experience now that I never understood before – one that truly surpasses all understanding – after hearing the words "You are terminal." (Technically, we are all; some of us just get the privilege of knowing how we will likely die, while the rest of you sit around and wonder.)

As Philippians 4:7 says: *"And the peace of God, which surpasses all understanding, will guard your hearts and your minds in Christ Jesus."* That peace is my anchor, keeping me steady when life feels overwhelming and uncertain. It's not something I could create on my own, but a gift God has graciously given me. And that same anchor—the one holding me firm—is the same one that will hold you close until it's your turn.

You don't have to be ready for the hard things, but staying close to God—through prayer, studying His Word, worship, and community—will sustain you. You just have to trust that God will meet you in there. And when He does, you'll discover a strength you never thought possible—not because of who you are, but because of who He is in you.

Practical Tools: Small, Everyday Practices for Resilience

One of my toxic traits is that I like to be in control. I like knowing what will happen next, how it's going to happen, what steps we're going to take, and what the outcome is going to be. In short, I like the 3-6 month plan. This is something I have had to work diligently on as I grow in my relationship with Christ. Now you know why I am put in these situations, like facing a semi. This is just one instance in my life (and there are many more) where I had zero control over the outcome. But God allowing me to face these situations reminds me that He is still in the driver's seat. He is still on the throne, and I get to trust Him to direct the steps. As you can tell, I am not always a quick learner. I am still facing these tough battles that remind me to trust Him every step of the way. However, I should note that I am diligent to always seek this growth as I desire to become more like Christ. It is through prayer, study of God's Word, and purposeful thanksgiving and gratitude that I feel I can stand up to the tests of each day and trust the outcome of each circumstance in my life, even if that means death.

Encouragement for Readers:

Although I would be quick to tell people to come to Christ, leave your troubles at the foot of the cross, pray, and get into His Word... I recognize this is easier said than done, especially through traumatic events or terminal diagnosis in our lives that may leave one angry with God. I know at seasons of my more immature walk with God, this would have been the answer I would have given.

I have a deep, exponential relationship with God, yet I found myself searching for a therapist who wasn't faith-based. That might seem counterproductive, right? At the time, I feared that a Christian therapist would simply tell me to read my Bible, pray, and trust that everything would be okay. But I was already a solid prayer warrior. I wasn't just reading the Bible—I was deeply engrossed in studying the Word of God. I had those spiritual disciplines in place, and while I am always growing, what I truly needed was healing.

For over a year, God had been nudging me to find a trauma counselor. These nudges came during a season when life was good. Everything felt stable—until it wasn't. Wisdom teaches us to obey when God calls us to a task, even if we don't fully understand why. If we don't schedule it, He will—often at the least convenient time. And that's exactly what happened. When tragedy struck, I wasn't prepared. The shock and additional pain made everything even harder to process. If I had listened sooner, if I had already found a therapist, it would have been like having the right medicine on the shelf—ready when I needed it most.

I finally surrendered to the constant poke and said, "Yes, God, who do I call?" After facing what should have been my last day on this side of Heaven, I woke up. I responded to God's nudge for me to seek a trauma therapist. That's because as we seek healing, He uses people, places, resources, medications, and so much more to bring about the healing His Word promises. I was trying to ignore the fact that I was in the Word, asking for God to send me a boat, and it turns out that boat remained anchored and waited for my heart to be ready. Meanwhile, God was nudging here and poking there, but I lacked the obedience. It was not because I was scared of therapy or had ill feelings toward it; rather, I was so busy and couldn't possibly see where I would fit in another appointment in my schedule. If things were okay, I totally believed the lie that I was fixed and I could leave it alone.

If you lack resilience in your own challenges, seek trauma therapy. Trauma has a way of blocking us from experiencing the fullness of God and the healing He desires to bestow on you. I have been seeing my therapist for two years at the time of writing this book. There is no way I could have faced the challenges of 2024 without taking the time and energy to heal from the many past traumas. Healing from your traumas allows you to hear God more clearly when you pray and seek His Word. Without healing, the weight of unresolved pain can make it almost impossible to hear from God about what needs to heal. Therapy is like insurance—it prepares you to receive healing when you need it most, rather than waiting until everything falls apart. It provides you with the coping skills necessary to take on the challenges promised to come your way in life. Healing allows you to experience a cup half full, seeing life with a heart of thanksgiving and many reasons to be grateful.

Resilience isn't just about pushing through—it's about healing, too.

For so long, I thought strength meant enduring, carrying the weight of my struggles without breaking. But real strength? It's in surrender. It's in learning that we don't have to hold everything alone. That sometimes, resilience looks like rest. Sometimes, faith looks like letting go. And sometimes, healing requires more than just prayer—it requires action.

So, what about you?

Are you carrying wounds you haven't allowed yourself to feel? Have you convinced yourself that survival is enough, when deep down, you know there's more? Have you ignored the nudge to seek healing because life is too busy, or because you're afraid of what you'll uncover?

Healing isn't a luxury—it's a necessity. Unhealed pain doesn't just sit quietly in the background; it shapes how we see ourselves, how we respond to others, and how we hear from God.

You don't have to wait for everything to fall apart to begin healing. I hate that I waited for the most tragic event in my life to seek trauma healing. I finally leaned into the process.

You also have this beautiful challenging work to uncover. Focus on growing in your relationship with Christ, and in His magnificence, God will reveal the right things in His perfect timing. If you begin the healing now, you'll be ahead of the game—better equipped to face whatever comes next.

I'll share what it looked like for me to finally lean into the process—the hard, messy, beautiful work of uncovering what I had buried. It wasn't easy. It wasn't instant. But it was necessary and it will be for you as well.

And maybe, just maybe, this is your nudge to begin that process, too.

Chapter 8

TRAUMA COUNSELING: THE DOOR TO HEALING

I thought I understood trauma. Over the years, I've faced my fair share—autoimmune diseases, the terrifying accident with my daughter, and the endless battles with my own body. But nothing prepared me for the slow unraveling that comes living with a terminal disease. For so long, I'd been in survival mode, managing the next appointment, the next crisis, the next piece of bad news. What I didn't realize was how much I was carrying inside me.

When my counselor first suggested we dive into the layers of trauma I'd accumulated, I resisted. I didn't want to unpack it all—I wasn't sure I could. But those sessions became a lifeline. Slowly, I learned to name the emotions I'd buried. I cried for the things I'd lost and the ones I was still losing. And through it all, I found a surprising freedom.

Counseling didn't erase my diagnosis or make life easier, but it gave me tools—ways to reclaim hope when everything felt hopeless. Breathing exercises to calm my mind, journaling to untangle my thoughts, and the reminder that I didn't have to face this alone. My healing wasn't about fixing what was broken; it was about learning to live with the pieces and finding beauty in the mosaic they formed.

First Session: The Start of Healing

I was very open to trauma therapy. God had been nudging me toward it even before the accident, so when the time came, I was quick to respond. It felt like a wake-up call—a chance to finally take the step I'd been putting off. I'd always advocated for counseling, but my struggle was finding the time. Can you imagine life being so busy that you can't even squeeze in another appointment?

In January 2023, I'll never forget my first session with Kim, my therapist. I walked in with my most toxic traits on full display. I told her, "Listen, I've got things to do, places to go, and I'm being held up by this incident. What can we do to get me through this as quickly as possible?" Two years later, Kim and I still laugh about my attitude during that first session. I know she must have thought, *Oh boy, this girl has a long road ahead.*

And she was right.

Now, therapy is an appointment I schedule on purpose. There will always be time for it.

Breakthrough Moments: When Healing Took Root

My doctor strongly recommended finding a therapist trained in EMDR (Eye Movement Desensitization and Reprocessing). I was intrigued after researching its benefits and eager to start. But my therapist wasn't ready to dive into EMDR right away. She explained that rushing into it could cause more harm than good, so we spent the first three months building trust, exploring my family dynamics, identifying my triggers, and unpacking my past.

It wasn't easy to slow down, but I trusted her process. She helped me see that grief isn't linear—it's messy, up and down, and breakthroughs happen along the way.

Early in therapy, I told Kim that I felt overwhelmed and incapable of continuing my business. I was ready to shut it down and take the simplest job I could find. Remember the McDonald's idea? I couldn't see how I could serve my clients while dealing with this trauma. Kim listened and said, "Why don't you slow down instead of quitting? It's okay if you don't meet all your goals this year. It's okay if all you do right now is keep the doors open and take one day at a time."

Those words were life-changing. I agreed to a four-week plan to be still—no big goals, no new clients, just small, manageable steps. By the end of those four weeks, I felt a peace I hadn't experienced in months. That year went on to be the highest sales revenue year for my business. It wasn't from pushing harder but from embracing healing.

Daily Tools: Resilience in Practice

Remember, Proverbs 3:5-6 has been my life verse: *"Trust in the Lord with all your heart; lean not on your own understanding. In all your ways acknowledge Him, and He will make your paths straight." (Mix of NIV and NKJV)* I memorized it as a new believer and held onto it during every challenge. But over time, I learned that trusting God doesn't mean avoiding life's battles—it means facing them with Him.

Another verse that has shaped me is Proverbs 16:9: *"In their hearts, humans plan their course, but the Lord establishes their steps."* These scriptures have taught me to surrender my need for control—a lesson I continue to learn every day.

These were my life verses. The two verses went hand in hand, covered by Isaiah 55:8-9: *"For my thoughts are not your thoughts, nor are your ways my ways," says the Lord."*

I wanted nothing more than to control everything around me. This was my toxic trait that would lead me to understanding the life verses God set before me. He knew I had this desire to control the outcomes of my life events. Up until now, I was able to take every life setback or hard event, and these verses brought me comfort. I became excellent at seeing the good even in the hard things because these verses were written on my heart.

Until I faced a semi.

My wheels were spinning on the ice. I looked around to see if I could run. You see, even in what would have been my last three seconds of life, I was still looking for a way to control the outcome. And for the first time ever, there was *nothing*—not a single thing I could do to change the outcome. It would have been the one thing that took my life.

One of the first revelations I had in trauma therapy, during one of my first EMDR sessions, was that I am not in control. Surprisingly, the accident was the last thing that came to mind—something that truly shocked me. In EMDR, you process whatever comes to mind first, and before I could even begin to work through the accident, my mind surfaced layers of past experiences, unresolved pain, and buried emotions that needed attention first. It was as if my heart knew there were deeper wounds to address before

I could face the trauma of the accident. Through it all, I came to realize that no matter how much I try to control a situation or plan the best path in life, God is ultimately the one in control. He is the one I trust, the one who directs my path, and the only one who knows the day or hour He will call me home.

Journaling and Scripture writing had been life practices I cultivated over the years that were always calming. When handwriting became increasingly difficult, my counselor encouraged me to use other methods, like talk-to-text tools, to keep writing my feelings and experiences down despite the struggles with my hands. Other tools she encouraged were deep breathing exercises, mindful meditations, staying active in prayer and Bible study, and connecting with friends and community. These tools covered everything from overcoming anxiety when I was alone to relaxing when I felt the urge to control what I couldn't. They helped me continue growing in character, understanding, and preventing social withdrawal—a common response after trauma.

Support for Others: Why Therapy Matters

Therapy is for everyone. Think of it like insurance—you don't wait until you're in an accident to get coverage. It's something you invest in now to prepare for the challenges life will inevitably bring. If I hadn't spent a year embracing trauma therapy leading up to this point, I wouldn't have been able to face a terminal diagnosis with the grace and ease that I did. But let me be clear—it was still not easy.

If you're unsure whether therapy is for you, remember this: life will throw curveballs. It's not a matter of "if" but "when." Having the coping skills in place before those moments come can make all the difference. Therapy isn't a sign of weakness; it's an act of strength. It equips you with the tools you need to face life's storms, and with the right counselor, it invites Him to come alongside you to find beauty on the other side.

Chapter 9

FINDING STRENGTH IN VULNERABILITY

For most of my life, I thought strength meant standing tall and keeping it together. But ALS has taught me that true strength comes from letting others in. The day I finally broke the news to my family, I expected fear, sadness, and maybe even anger. What I didn't expect was the overwhelming support that poured in.

When I started sharing my journey on social media, it wasn't to inspire anyone. It was because I needed to speak my truth. I didn't anticipate the way it would connect me to others—people I'd never met who reached out with love, prayers, and their own stories of struggle. Vulnerability isn't a weakness; it's a bridge.

Allowing others to see my pain, my joy, and my fears opened doors I never knew existed. It also connected me with families who let me in and allowed me to walk alongside them. Recently, three people I met online—two devoted caregivers who lost their loved ones and one fellow ALS fighter who passed—have been heavy on my heart.

I learned to ask for help when I needed it and to accept it with grace. In sharing my story, I found that it gave others permission to share theirs, to reflect on their own beliefs, and to seek deeper understanding. There's a surprising strength in vulnerability—it connects us, binds us to one another, and reminds us that we're never truly alone.

Opening Up

When I was first diagnosed with ALS, I had no idea what this disease was. Of course, I researched it right away and discovered there was no cure. There was no way out of this situation. This was the ultimate inability to control anything, and the test was more real than it had ever been before.

As I learned about ALS, I discovered there wasn't a true test to diagnose the disease. Instead, there was a set of criteria that had to be met, and the EMG was a great tool for confirming it. This allowed denial to sit at the forefront of my mind. The physical changes and struggles I was facing were very obvious now, and my ability to work was diminishing. I had to be honest about what I was facing.

At the same time, being honest about this diagnosis meant the possibility of being wrong. Can you imagine telling the world you are dying, only to find out the doctors were mistaken and perhaps had discovered something fully treatable? I could have kept this to myself, but I saw an opportunity to share my faith through my journey. I let my guard down. I used my growing social media platforms to share the ups and downs, the ins and outs. Behind the scenes, I was always afraid of having to come to my community and say, "We got it wrong."

Would I lose the trust of others? Would people who had come to know the Lord through my story lose their newfound faith?

Over time, I began to see that people weren't discovering their faith because of my diagnosis specifically, but rather through the faith, hope, and joy I had despite the challenges I faced in life.

It took a lot of courage for me to create that first post sharing my diagnosis, but here we are a year later. My body is failing me as expected. The many people who have grown in their faith, found Jesus for the first time, or returned to their faith because of my testimony cannot be counted.

God answered my prayers as a believer. I wanted to be a missionary from day one. I thought that meant packing my bags and traveling across the world to tell everyone about Jesus and what He had done to save me. Over the years, I established communities across social and online platforms, as well as within my churches and neighborhoods. I never imagined how God would use those platforms to install a mission quite like this. In facing a terminal disease, He gave me a global reach, and I never had to pack a bag.

Connections Made

As a believer, I've learned that the church doesn't always love the way Jesus loves. We live in a time where disciples believe their primary role is to point out public sins while failing to recognize their own.

In 2008, I worked with a younger girl who became a close friend. We were both pregnant at the same time and delivered premature babies around the same time. We connected on so many levels. After delivering my fourth child at 32 weeks, I began questioning whether I could return to work. My husband preferred I stay home with our babies—now four kids under five years old.

While on maternity leave, I had a literal "come to Jesus" moment. Nobody was ministering to me, I wasn't hanging out with anyone sharing their faith, and nobody prayed for my salvation. Yet, on a Thursday, I had that moment. I'll never forget it.

Although my growing faith separated me from some of those friendships over time, social media allowed me to stay connected with this friend. She went on to marry and have two more children.

Over the years, I learned that we didn't share the same religious or political views. But I was never the friend to block or unfriend over such differences. I appreciated that others had different upbringings and worldviews. That understanding allowed me to focus on loving others rather than trying to convince them to see things my way.

A Conversation That Changed Everything

On January 1, 2025, I received a private message from this friend. It was through my vulnerability, and my willingness to stay resilient, even while facing my own exit from the world, that my testimony reached her in a profound way. After she "unsent" her first two messages, she finally found the words.

I want to share this conversation with you. My hope is that it will show how living out your faith can reach others for Christ—more than judgment or condemnation ever could. Before the threat of hell convinces anyone, before constant nagging changes their perspective, simply living authentically and loving openly can make the greatest impact. This conversation is a testament to the power of vulnerability and the work of the Holy Spirit when we simply love.

Anonymous: *"I cannot even tell you how many times I've thought about writing you this message, but I kept deciding, 'I'll do it later. There's time.' Who am I kidding though? There's not always time. I remember seeing your Facebook post when you announced your diagnosis. I knew what ALS is, but didn't know a lot about it aside from Stephen Hawking, so the first thing I did was Google 'ALS life expectancy.'*

You know all too well the harsh information I found. You see, one of the biggest fears I have is dying, and since seeing your diagnosis post, I find myself quickly skimming or even just scrolling right past your posts and TikToks. I'm not like you. I don't necessarily believe in God or heaven.

My fear is the unknown of what happens after death. Do you just cease to exist? Does your 'spirit' just float around aimlessly? Is there even any kind of afterlife? See what I mean? No one REALLY knows, and if I don't acknowledge it, it's not real, right? This is why I kept putting off writing you.

Telling you all about my fear of death seems like such a selfish thing when you are the one facing it nose to nose. But knowing you (and I feel like I know you decently well despite our distance these last 15ish years), I think you'd like to hear these things from me.

One question I have for you though is, are you angry at all? I am SO mad that such a beautiful light like yourself is having your time here cut short, and in all the skimming I have done on your posts and TikToks, you are always so positive, and I just don't understand it.

Okay. I'm sorry for the novel, but if I didn't get it all out at once, I don't think I would have gotten it out at all, and then I would have regretted it (more of my selfishness showing there haha). I'm terrified of dying, and I don't understand how you aren't. I have many fond memories of you and think of you often.

I'm definitely jealous of your seemingly unwavering faith in your religion. You will always have a place in my heart! Nothing but love for you, girl."

Deanna: *"Even years apart, I still care deeply for you, and that will never change. We go back... way back... I totally understand the trigger, and that's why you scroll past as quickly as you can. I think we all do that with things that trigger us—it's a trauma response. Regardless of what we believe, none of us will make it out of here alive. The hardest part is not having the 3–6-month plan.*

Deanna's unspoken thought: I understand this all too well, right? It's that toxic trait I have—the one that likes to be in control of every outcome.

But if we had all the details, we would literally be scared to live each day to the fullest because we'd know what's coming. Even with all religious beliefs aside, I think it may be really helpful to hear that perspective. I believe death is equally as beautiful as birth. We were born to serve our purpose in the world, and to have the Lord say, 'Mission complete,' is a blessing.

Am I angry? Not at all... but I do get scared sometimes. I'm afraid of the pains that come with dying. I'm managing the 'Braxton Hicks,' as I like to call it, with morphine and Ativan. That helps reduce my fear of the pain.

It's been a struggle to think, why me at 43? I have a great marriage and amazing kids. It's been a long road to understanding and acceptance. I've come to understand that the Lord blessed me with my children, but they were His children all along. He trusted me to lead, teach, and guide them, and I sought to be obedient to that. There will be parts of their journey, growth they will experience, and lives they will change that wouldn't happen if I were still here.

Bringing children into the world is exciting and filled with joy. Although dying comes with grief, I believe it's meant to be equally as beautiful.

Time here—on this side of heaven—makes it feel so daunting and long. What I do know without a doubt is that something in your life will happen that will begin shifting your perspective and help you find peace with the fact that one day you will die too.

Let this be the reason you live every day to the fullest. Take lots of pictures and videos even if others don't like it. Take that vacation even if you can't afford it. You can't get back opportunities to make memories and spend time with those you love. I spent two years purposely making memories and spending time with my kids before my diagnosis. I don't believe that was an accident. It was preparing me for what was to come.

I've experienced some things that have shaped my unwavering beliefs, and I know you will find yourself doing the same—maybe even now as you try to understand your trauma responses to death and dying. In the end, our beliefs may differ because your experiences and worldview differ from mine, and that's okay."

Anonymous: "Okay, now that I'm done crying. One of my favorite things about you is that you don't judge ANYONE for any reason. Living deep in the Bible Belt now, I learned pretty quickly that not everyone who claims to *love Jesus is nice when they find out I do not share their beliefs. Never, for even a second, did I worry you would condemn me for that!*

I can understand your comparison of death to birth. Birth can be so traumatic, and messy, painful, and scary... just like death. Shoot, who's to say we weren't somewhere else before we were born in this life? I would LOVE to feel the same way about it, and maybe someday I will. Love you SO much!"

***

The Power of Love

So many may feel as though I missed an opportunity to win her salvation in Jesus. So many Christians would have taken this moment to start preaching, in turn pushing the seeker away. But I believe He is already using my story, my testimony, and my unwavering faith to allow her to question her fears and beliefs.

All I had to do was love her. That love displayed will keep her heart and mind open as the Holy Spirit continues working in her life.

Strength in Sharing: The Power of Letting People See Your Pain and Joy

Authenticity was the most important core value I lived by. To be authentic meant being true to my personality, morals, values, and beliefs, despite any influence or pressure to be otherwise. My faith, however, wasn't always my own.

What do I mean by that? As a new believer, I was captivated by the women in my church who seemed to have grown to unimaginable depths in their walk with God. They wore long dresses, had their hair tied back in neat ponytails, homeschooled their perfect children, never said a cuss word, home-cooked every meal, cleaned their homes before their husbands came home from work, and even removed their husbands' shoes for them. Okay, some of that might be exaggerated, but I admired them so much that I started changing myself to become more like them.

While I was growing in God's Word, I lacked the confidence to defend my spunky self and follow God at the same time. I'm not sure some of those women would have known how to handle me if they'd seen the real me—the one who chose Jesus as her Savior but wasn't willing to compromise the unique, vibrant person God created. That version of me was spunky, bold, and unapologetic.

Over the years, I kept trying to live up to what I thought the church wanted me to be. I felt like I was always trying to keep up with the stay-at-home, homeschooling moms who built their lives around their husbands. I even felt guilty if I didn't wake up to make my husband breakfast. The problem? I am not, nor have I ever been, a morning person. To this day, I'm still not a morning person. If I do get up to make breakfast for my husband, I won't be doing it with a cheerful heart!

I'm fully convinced that if God wanted me to see the sunrise, He would've scheduled it for 8 a.m.

All jokes aside, many of the women around me seemed like perfect Proverbs 31 wives, and I constantly struggled to be like them.

In 2019, I had a revelation: I wasn't showing up authentically in my life. I know I reached people along the way, and I know God was using me, but suddenly, I realized it was okay to be *me*.

You can see the difference in the pictures from before 2019 and after 2020. While photos don't always tell the whole story, I can see a clear transformation. Before, I was trying to be someone else; afterward, I surrendered and allowed God to use the *me* He created. That's when I truly showed up.

Letting people experience my ups and downs, my wins and losses, has given them a glimpse of what authenticity looks like. Some of those women I admired along the way—the ones I thought had perfect lives—now make me wonder if they only seemed so perfect because they were hiding behind life's challenges, afraid of being judged.

Being vulnerable about my life has allowed others to see the one thing we can truly control: our responses to the challenges we face. Finding my authentic self and living in the traits God gifted me with has created more revival around me than all the years I spent trying to be someone I wasn't.

Social Media Impact: Vulnerability's Unexpected Blessings

Allowing others to witness our challenges and painful experiences gives them a front-row seat to the power of God when He performs miracles or answers prayers.

Throughout my life, I've met people who are deeply private yet have incredible testimonies. Sometimes, they are so private that I feel as though their miracles or answered prayers go unnoticed. I know it's never truly wasted, but I wonder how many others could have been encouraged or inspired if they'd shared their stories.

Of course, I remind myself that I am not like them. I am anything *but* quiet—maybe even a little over the top at times. But y'all, I do not want to throw away an opportunity to win someone over for Christ. That's why I've used my social media platforms not only as a way to journal my journey but also to share my life in a way that impacts others.

Since being diagnosed with ALS, sharing my end-of-life journey on social media has brought countless blessings that far outweigh the challenges. When others see God show up in my life—when they witness peace that surpasses all understanding, the kind of peace they know they've never experienced—it prompts them to ask, "How do you feel this peace?"

When people see answers to prayer, when they witness the impossible becoming possible, it forces them to ask questions about where such peace and joy come from.

More than 70% of the people who comment on or share my posts are strangers—people I've never met in real life. Isn't that fascinating? Of course, my family and close friends are impacted, but knowing my story is reaching people I'll never meet reminds me that I'm doing a global work simply by sharing the ups and downs of living with a terminal disease.

Every time someone is encouraged by my story or feels inspired to seek the Lord, I know that sharing my vulnerability has fulfilled a purpose greater than I could have ever imagined.

Healing isn't just about what happens inside of us—it's also about what happens when we allow others in.

Vulnerability has a way of opening doors we never expected—inviting connection, deepening relationships, and leaving an impact far beyond ourselves.

Sharing my journey wasn't always easy, but it became clear that when we let others see our struggles, we also give them permission to find hope in their own. But now, as I step into this next part of my journey, my perspective shifts again. This isn't just about living—it's about preparing for what comes next.

Death used to feel like a thief, but now I see it differently. It's not the end—it's a transition. And what I do with the time between now and then is entirely up to me. So, let's talk about it. Let's talk about life, about death, and about the kind of legacy we leave behind. Because when we embrace both with intention, we find something unexpected—joy, even in the hardest places.

The Hunt for the Bougie Diapers

No one ever tells you that adulthood might involve a full-blown crisis over diaper quality, but here I am.

It all started with an itch—right in the most inconvenient place possible. My butt crack. At first, I thought, Okay, annoying, but manageable. But then I realized something was wrong. Like, really wrong. A chunk of my skin had straight-up abandoned ship. Cue full-blown meltdown mode.

I yanked myself out of bed, grabbed my cane like I was heading into battle, and hobbled to the bathroom at record speed. One look in the mirror and I was convinced—this was it. A bed sore. The beginning of the end. Forget ALS; this was how I was going out. Rhianna, my daughter-in-law and certified CNA, was there when I burst out of the bathroom like a madwoman. She took one look at my crisis situation and, in her calm, professional way, basically told me I was being dramatic.

"It's just a scratch," she said.

"JUST A SCRATCH?" I gasped. "DO YOU SEE THE CHUNK OF SKIN MISSING?"

She sighed, grabbed some butt paste, and got to work like this was just another Tuesday.

"Hold still. This will help," she said, slathering it on.
Now, listen. I don't just let any mystery goop get applied to my delicate regions without some serious questioning.

The Hunt for the Bougie Diapers, con't. . .

"Wait a minute," I said, eyeing the tube. "What exactly is that?"
"Butt paste," Rhianna replied, not even looking up.

"But what's in it?" I demanded. "Because if I start glowing or
develop some kind of superpower, I need to know what we're
working with here."

"It's got colloidal silver," she said.
I froze. "So you're telling me my butt is about to turn into a
precious metal?!"
"No, it helps with healing."

Well, that was a relief. And, to be fair, it actually did help. Within
hours, the itch and the burning started to fade. My poor, suffering
backside was on the road to recovery.

But there was still one major problem: The diapers had betrayed me.
This wasn't just an isolated incident. Oh no. This was a pattern. I
had tried multiple brands, and all of them had left me itchy,
miserable, and mildly traumatized. I needed a solution.

Thus began The Great Bougie Diaper Hunt.

I scoured the internet like a woman on a mission. I read reviews. I
researched materials. I briefly considered launching a full-scale
scientific experiment with charts, spreadsheets, and a ranking
system. Did I need organic cotton? Bamboo? NASA-grade moisture-
wicking technology? Was there such a thing as Gucci diapers?

The Hunt for the Bougie Diapers, con't. . .

Because at this point, I was willing to invest.

And yet... nothing.

So, if you ever see me in the adult diaper aisle, holding a package like it personally wronged me, just know—I'm still on the hunt.

– Deanna

A New Lens on Life and Death, Part 4

Death used to feel like a thief—something that came uninvited, stealing what I held dear.

For so long, I feared it. I fought against it. I saw it as something distant—something I'd deal with someday. But with ALS shaping my days, I see it differently now. Death is not an end; it's a transition. And what lies between now and then? That's entirely up to me.

Maybe you've feared death too—not just the physical ending, but the loss of time, the what-ifs, the regrets. Maybe you've avoided thinking about it altogether, believing there's always more time.

But what if—just for a moment—you allowed yourself to ask:

- What would I do differently if I knew my time was running out?

- Am I truly living, or just existing?

- Have I filled my days with what matters most?

This next part of my journey isn't about giving up—it's about choosing how I live regardless of how many days are left. It's about finding joy, making memories, and embracing each breath as a gift. It's about looking at life and death through a lens of hope, humor, and faith.

Because the truth is, you don't have to be dying to start living with purpose.

So as we step into these final chapters together, I invite you to look at your own life through a new lens. Not one of fear, but of gratitude. Not one of scarcity, but of abundance.

Because even in the shadow of death, there is room for laughter, love, and purpose.

Let's begin.

Chapter 10

FINDING JOY IN THE END-OF-LIFE JOURNEY

The room is full, a mix of quiet sobs and soft laughter as stories are shared about my life. The atmosphere is heavy, but then—just as the service seems to be winding down—Kori stands up, smoothing out her dress, a mischievous glint in her eye. She takes a deep breath, gives a heartfelt speech, and just as everyone is expecting some final, tearful words—she turns around, lifts a bouquet high in the air, and tosses it over her shoulder.

"You're next!" she announces with a grin.

The room falls silent for a split second before nervous laughter erupts, some guests gasping in surprise, others catching the joke immediately. It's dark humor at its finest, and exactly the kind of send-off I would have wanted.

Because here's the thing—I don't want my funeral to be a place of just sadness. I want it to be a reflection of my life, full of love, laughter, and the kind of humor that catches you off guard and makes you snort-laugh in the middle of an otherwise serious moment. ALS may be taking my body, but it will never take my spirit. And if I can find humor even in death, then maybe—just maybe—you can find a little joy in the unexpected, too.

I used to think of death as something to fear—something dark and cold. But now, with ALS shaping my days, I see it differently—like a promise, not a punishment. Celebratory equal to birth. It hasn't always been easy to get here. There were nights I was angry, nights I cried, and days when the weight of this disease threatened to crush me. But in those moments, something unexpected kept me going: HUMOR!

Yes, humor. Even when I couldn't run or even walk fast anymore, I'd find ways to laugh. Like the time I tried to dance at a wedding, knowing full well my legs would cramp afterward.

Humor is my way of telling this disease it won't steal my spirit, even if it takes my body.

But it's more than laughter. It's the peace I've found in small moments—watching my kids grow, making diamond art, and just sitting quietly with God. I've learned to see life as a series of gifts, not guarantees. I pray for peace, for joy, for the strength to make memories that matter—not for more days. I don't need more time; I need better time.

ALS didn't give me a choice in how this ends, but it's given me the chance to choose how I live. And let me tell you, there's joy even here, in this place I never thought I'd find it.

Unexpected Joy: Small Moments That Mean Everything

My hair appointments are a necessity. I've been seeing the same hairstylist, Kori, since moving back to Wyoming in 2020. Kori is truly amazing, and I enjoy every moment I spend in her chair. We share a similar sense of dark humor—something that makes old people cringe but keeps us in stitches.

We've even made plans like stealing my best friend's hideous old funeral dress named Irma (and trust me, it's *ugly*). She's been wearing it to funerals since I met her, but she's definitely not wearing it to mine! We've schemed to steal it from her closet, wrap it up in a gift box, and include a card from me that says, "You weren't wearing that to my funeral!"

Then there's the plan to have Kori text people from my phone during my funeral with messages like, "It's dark in here!"

Kori brings so much life to me, and I value her skills just as much as her humor. My hair always looks amazing because of her. She helps me balance my spunky personality with a professional look. I swore I'd never miss a hair appointment—if someone had to carry me into the salon, so be it!

But over Thanksgiving 2024, I began noticing a new level of decline. By early December, I lost my 20-year-old niece, who was medically complex and fought a good fight. After spending nearly four days at the hospital, completely out of my routine with nurses and caregivers, I thought I just needed rest.

I was so weak that I couldn't attend the private family viewing of my niece. When my hospice nurse came that day, she noticed my lungs were severely diminished and prescribed strict rest. She told me to focus on attending my niece's funeral and nothing else. By the following week, I worsened and was diagnosed with aspiration pneumonia.

That week, I missed my first hair appointment in nearly five years. I was so sick I didn't even care. Missing my appointment was completely out of character. It hit me hard, and it hit Kori even harder.

Dianna, my caregiver and best friend, and I usually go to our hair appointments together. For my December appointment, Dianna went alone. Kori knew something was wrong. It was a defining moment of truth about my health. She knew I didn't miss hair appointments.

Kori could have handled my absence differently. She could have charged me a missed appointment fee. Instead, she went above and beyond. She ordered an inflatable headrest online, came to my house, and replaced the headrest on my wheelchair with the inflatable one so she could do my hair right in my kitchen.

This act of kindness reminded me how people in our lives step up to the plate during our hardest seasons. It wasn't just about the hair—it was about someone showing up, understanding what brings me joy, and going the extra mile. That moment became a memory I'll always cherish.

Using Humor: A Coping Mechanism That Never Fails

Keeping my sense of humor alive has been an intentional goal from the day of my diagnosis. People often feel conflicted about how to act around someone who is terminal. They worry about laughing at the wrong time or asking questions that might offend.

I didn't want anyone to walk on eggshells around me. I decided to set the tone myself!

At the end of October, I ordered my daughter and husband Apple Watches on Amazon. The delivery was made by an Amazon Flex driver. I arrived home about 20 minutes after the package was delivered, according to our camera footage. When I wheeled up to the door, the box was opened, and both watches were gone. I was furious.

That day, I learned a new Amazon warehouse had opened in our small, rural area. After filing a police report and submitting it to Amazon, I spent two frustrating weeks fighting for a refund. I vowed to never order from Amazon again and took to social media to air my grievances.

Despite my vow, I survived the Christmas season without touching Amazon. But my bitterness lingered.

In January, I finally decided to order an urn I'd been eyeing on Amazon. I couldn't resist sharing my decision on social media, writing: "If my new urn gets stolen, I hope the thief needs it before I do."

Out of 100+ reactions and comments on my post, only four people got the joke. My friend Cassidy's comment won the day: "Worst case scenario, you can go in the empty box if they leave it at the door again."

I laughed so hard I almost peed my pants. That comment *won the internet* for me. Moments like that remind me why humor matters so much—it's not just a distraction; it's a lifeline.

Defining Joy: The Difference Between Fleeting Happiness and Deeper Joy

Fleeting happiness is the kind of happiness I chased through the whirlwind of life. It's a quick high, often tied to achieving goals, dreams, or accomplishments. It's those momentary pleasures we all experience—a burst of satisfaction that fades as quickly as it arrives. This surface-level happiness depends on external circumstances, leaving us craving the next accolade or accomplishment to fill the void.

The deeper joy I've discovered through past traumas, my terminal diagnosis, and this end-of-life journey is unshakable. It's rooted in something far more profound: resilience. This joy comes from embracing life's challenges and finding purpose in those difficult moments. It's about finding meaning in relationships, cherishing the small moments, and recognizing the raw beauty of simply waking up each day with breath in my lungs.

This deeper joy thrives even in the face of loss, pain, and uncertainty. It's not about escaping reality but leaning into it with resilience, grit, grace, faith, and the understanding that every breath—no matter how numbered—is a gift to be cherished.

"One day you will tell your story of how you overcame what you went through, and it will become someone else's survival guide." —Brené Brown

Practical Advice: Finding Joy in Your Own Challenges

Finding joy in the midst of challenges ultimately comes down to perspective and how we choose to react. It's about deciding whether to see the glass as half full or half empty. Life is full of circumstances we cannot control, but our response is always within our power.

Recently, I faced a situation that was completely out of my control. A friend who was helping with fundraising for my family made an awful decision to steal money from the fundraisers. When I discovered this betrayal, I was terrified to confront the situation.

There were fears of losing friends, and I knew the truth could take a long time to come out, especially given how slow the justice system can be. Part of me wanted to ignore it, to pretend it never happened. But my counselor helped me understand that this wasn't just about stolen money or wrongfully collected funds—it was about the impact on the people who had generously donated.

This perspective shift was significant. It became clear that justice was needed not just for my family but also for those who were defrauded.

The Weight of Forgiveness

When this all unfolded, a verse weighed heavily on me:

"Judge not, and you shall not be judged. Condemn not, and you shall not be condemned. Forgive, and you will be forgiven. Give, and it will be given to you: good measure, pressed down, shaken together, and running over will be put into your bosom. For with the same measure that you use, it will be measured back to you." —Luke 6:37–38

In my human nature, I wanted to judge her. Anytime I've sought to judge others, though, this verse reminds me to pause. It forces me to ask, "If I judge with this measure, am I prepared for that judgment to be measured back to me?"

This always makes me look within myself first.

A Hard Lesson in Trust

This theft situation put me between a rock and a hard place. The money was a gift anyway—maybe I should just be thankful for what we received. But the evidence continued to pile up. My counselor reminded me that this wasn't about judging someone; it was about holding them accountable.

When I confided in her, she explained that as a mandatory reporter, she was required to report the evidence I provided. There were clear crimes potentially committed here. I wanted to believe my friend's heart was in the right place, but the more I uncovered, the more it became clear that she had used my terminal diagnosis for personal gain.

My counselor's wisdom brought me peace. She explained that while I was focused on avoiding judgment, I needed to understand that sometimes we become victims through no fault of our own. This wasn't my burden to bear.

Finding Purpose Amid the Pain

The investigator warned me this could be a long road—filled with evidence gathering, accusations, and charges. I knew I would lose friendships, some of which had lasted more than 15 years. I felt like the bad guy.

But I began praying for the Lord to restore what had been lost—for Him to redeem my time, energy, and peace. As I prayed, God showed me that this situation had purpose. He gave me a mission: to speak out for those who are voiceless, especially vulnerable adults who are often victims of financial crimes.

This wasn't how I imagined my end-of-life journey would unfold, but it was real. And through it, I found joy in knowing my story could protect and prevent others from experiencing the same pain.

Choosing Joy

I hope you can see how to find joy in your own challenges, even when the circumstances feel impossible. It all comes down to how we choose to react.

If you see the glass as half empty, you'll focus on what's missing or what has been taken from you. This perspective leads to bitterness, anger, hopelessness, and feeling stuck.

But when you see the glass as half full, you'll notice the blessings that remain, even in the hardest moments. This doesn't mean ignoring the pain or pretending everything is perfect—it means recognizing that even in hardship, there is still good to be found.

Joy is not the absence of hardship but the ability to find light within it. You cannot always control what happens to you, but you can control how you react. Choosing to look for the best in life's challenges and responding with gratitude—that is where true joy resides.

So the question is—are you making the moments that will truly matter?

In the next chapter, I'll share how I became intentional about creating memories—not someday, but now. Because when time is limited, you realize that every moment is a chance to leave something behind that lasts.

Chapter 11

MEMORIES THAT MATTER

One of the hardest lessons I've learned is how fleeting life can be. Every moment we get is a gift, and I've stopped wasting them. After my diagnosis, I made it a priority to create meaningful memories with the people I love. Not later. Not someday. Now.

We've taken trips—family vacations to the Bahamas and quiet moments on the porch. I've poured my heart into small goals, like finishing my diamond art projects to raise money for scholarships. I've stopped letting guilt over money or time get in the way. These memories are my legacy.

I've also become fiercely intentional about my relationships. I talk openly with my family about what's coming, even the hard parts, like hospice and end-of-life care. I tell them, "Don't be afraid to let me go. Don't feel guilty for putting me in a facility if that's what's best. Just come and visit. Be with me."

And it's not just the big conversations. It's the small, everyday moments that stick—the times my kids and I laugh over something silly, the late-night talks with my husband. Those are the treasures I'm leaving behind.

Every memory we make is a way of saying, "I was here, and I loved you." That's all I want for the people I leave behind: to know they were deeply, truly loved.

Legacy Moments: Memories to Treasure Forever

I received a preliminary diagnosis of ALS on January 12, 2024. By then, mimicking diseases had been ruled out, and my spine doctor was 95% sure of the diagnosis. We still had to complete the EMG, the best diagnostic tool for ALS today.

On January 31, 2024, my spine doctor completed my EMG, and I received a definite ALS diagnosis. I jumped into learning everything I could—joining ALS groups, ordering recommended books, and connecting with Jennifer, a mentor whose husband has ALS. She gave me incredible guidance, but she warned me not to immerse myself in forums or books unless my diagnosis was confirmed.

One of the most important pieces of advice I received early on was this: Book those family trips. Don't waste a moment.

I couldn't fully grasp the importance of that advice at first, but I'm so thankful I acted on it. Within six weeks of my diagnosis, I started booking a cruise, family reunions, and trips to visit loved ones across the country.

I remember questioning myself while booking our cruise: "Am I doing this too soon? What if I've been misdiagnosed? What will people think if I spend money on these trips and end up getting better?"

Then, I shifted my perspective. We are all going to die. None of us will make it out of here alive. My time might come before yours, but your time will come too. I asked myself, "Will I ever regret spending this time with my family?"

The answer was clear: No. Regardless of the outcome, I knew I would never regret those moments together.

Seven months post-diagnosis, I was no longer able to travel. Looking back, I'm so grateful I didn't let fear or denial guide me. Memories were made, and hospice was recommended less than a week before I took my final trip.

Big and Small Moments: The Ones That Stay

Life is full of big milestones and small, quiet moments, and I've learned to cherish them all.

One of the most significant memories I've created was our family cruise. It was a beautiful experience filled with laughter, togetherness, and unforgettable scenery. The time spent on that trip reminded me of how precious and fleeting these moments are.

But it's not just the big trips that matter. It's the small, everyday memories that I treasure just as much. Like the quiet evenings spent talking with my husband or laughing with my kids over something silly. Those moments may seem insignificant at the time, but they're the ones that stick.

Intentionality: Living for Today

To make these memories, I had to become intentional. No more waiting for "someday" or letting excuses hold me back. I stopped worrying about whether I could afford the time or money for trips and instead asked myself one question: "Will I regret not doing this?"

That simple shift in perspective changed everything.

If you're not sure whether you should book that trip, spend that time, or make that memory, ask yourself the same question: "Will I regret this?" If the answer is no, then make it happen.

You don't have to be dying to start making memories with the people you love. Take the first step, make the deposit, and watch God work.

Encouragement: Finding Time for What Matters

To anyone who feels too busy to create meaningful memories with loved ones: life will always be busy. There will always be deadlines, bills, and responsibilities pulling at your time. But those things will fade, while the memories you make will last forever.

It's not about waiting for the perfect time. It's about choosing to prioritize the people and moments that matter most.

A Final Thought

Memories are our way of saying, "I was here, and I loved you." Don't wait. Take the trip. Laugh at the silly moments. Have the hard conversations. Cherish every breath and every second you're given with the people you love.

Because in the end, those memories aren't just for us—they're for the ones we leave behind.

In the next chapter, I'll share how faith has shaped my journey, how hope has carried me, and how leaving a legacy is about so much more than what we leave—it's about how we live.

Chapter 12

FAITH, HOPE AND LEAVING A LEGACY

In the early days of my diagnosis, I had a conversation with God that shifted everything. He asked me, *"Do you still believe what you said you believed?"* And I answered, *"Yes, Lord. I'm still not afraid to die."*

But getting to that place wasn't easy. After the car accident that nearly killed me the year before my diagnosis, I felt betrayed by God. I wondered, *Why save me then, only to let me face this now?* I wrestled with that anger, grappling with questions that seemed to have no answers.

Then, through scripture and prayer, God showed me something: He didn't save me to punish me. He saved me to give me time—time to say goodbye, to make memories, and to love well.

I remember Hezekiah in the Bible and see a reflection of my own journey. Hezekiah pleaded with God for more time, and God granted it. His prayer resonates with me: *"Remember, Lord, how I have walked before you faithfully and with wholehearted devotion"* (2 Kings 20:3, NIV). God granted him fifteen more years, and while my extension might not be as long, it's still a gift.

This time hasn't been about fighting against death but embracing life. I've stopped pleading for physical healing and started recognizing the healing in my soul. God has been restoring my heart, giving me a peace that surpasses understanding.

To those who've prayed for my healing, I want you to know that your prayers are felt, cherished, and answered—just not in the way you might have expected. My miracle isn't in the prolonging of my life. My miracle is the unshakable peace I've found. That is the greatest healing of all.

When I was first diagnosed with ALS, I thought my race had hit its final stretch. But as the months passed, I realized this journey wasn't about the finish line—it was about how I ran the last leg.

Living with a terminal illness isn't the death sentence people imagine. It's an invitation to live with purpose and intention. It's about embracing every breath as a victory and every day as a gift.

I've found hope in the simplest routines: prayer, scripture, and the steady presence of God. I've found joy in the unexpected—like dark humor shared with friends or the quiet stillness of a morning spent with my kids. These moments aren't grand, but they are full of meaning.

Hope and joy coexist with pain. They're not about denying the reality of my diagnosis but finding beauty in it. Resilience isn't about avoiding the storm; it's about finding purpose within it. Even when I feel weak, I remember: *"But those who hope in the Lord will renew their strength. They will soar on wings like eagles"* (Isaiah 40:31, NIV).

To those in the last stretch of their journey, I'd say this: Don't focus on what you're losing. Focus on what you can still give. Your time, your presence, your love—that's where purpose lives. The legacy you leave will be etched in the hearts of those you've touched, not in the number of your days.

Legacy isn't about the material things we leave behind. It's about the love we pour into others and the memories that outlive us.

For me, legacy is connection. It's my children knowing how deeply they were loved, my husband remembering our quiet conversations, and my friends holding onto the laughter we shared. It's the lessons I've passed down—the ones that remind them to choose love, grace, and resilience, no matter what life throws their way.

I've spent hours writing letters to my children. Each one is filled with my hopes for their futures, my prayers for their happiness, and the memories I'll always cherish. I've recorded messages for milestones I won't see—not to cling to what I'll miss, but to ensure they feel my presence even after I'm gone.

My mother left me with a legacy of kindness and faith. She didn't give me riches, but she gave me wisdom, strength, and love. That's the legacy I hope to leave—a reminder that even in life's hardest moments, love is what endures.

To my readers, I say this: You don't have to wait for a terminal diagnosis to build a legacy of love. Start today. Be present. Forgive. Pour your heart into the people you love, and let them feel it in every hug, every laugh, and every moment you share.

"I have fought the good fight, I have finished the race, I have kept the faith," **2 Timothy 4:7**

Conclusion

LIVING SO YOU'RE READY TO DIE

This journey has taught me that living well is the secret to dying well. It's not about how much time we have, but how we use it.

I've learned to redefine resilience—not as the absence of struggle, but as the courage to face it with grace. I've learned to find joy, not in what I can do, but in who I can be for others. And I've learned to live with purpose so that when the time comes, I can let go in peace.

Death isn't the enemy. Fear is. And I refuse to let fear steal the joy of my final days. The world has sold us the lie that death is something to be feared, but I see it differently now.

To you, my reader, my prayer is simple: Live so you're ready to die. Celebrate the little moments. Love deeply. Forgive freely. Say the words that matter today, not tomorrow.

The finish line isn't the end; it's the beginning of something greater. And as I cross it, I go with hope, joy, and the belief that life's greatest gift isn't how long we live, but how deeply we love.

If the Lord chooses to heal me on this side of Heaven, we will shout it from the rooftops that He is the ultimate healer. But if He chooses to heal me in the hands of Jesus, the healing is the same.

Either way—I AM HEALED.

The Great Catheter Catastrophe:
A Tale of Pee, Pride, and Betrayal

I knew I had a call with my publisher, so I needed my proof copy—the one where I had scribbled all my brilliant, life-changing notes. But could I find it? Of course not. I found two other copies that other people had read, but not mine. My book, my notes, my genius? Nowhere to be found.

Determined, I got out of bed, grabbed my catheter bag and cane, and started pacing around my room, determined to track it down. I looked under things, over things, in places that made no sense at all —because let's be real, sometimes objects disappear into some alternate dimension just to mess with you.

Then, finally—victory! I spotted it sitting on my side table, exactly where I should have looked first. Feeling accomplished, I moved the table out of the way and prepared for my grand return to bed.

Now, in my head, I was about to execute this move with grace and ease. I jumped up, and my first leg landed perfectly on the bed. But just as my second leg went to follow...

SNAP.

Oh no. Oh, no no no. I knew that sound. And it was not good. That was my catheter line breaking.

For a split second, I thought, Maybe I can fix this myself. Maybe it just came loose, and I could snap it back together real quick, and no one would ever have to know.

Then, I felt it.

The Great Catheter Catastrophe: Con't...

Warm. Unmistakable. Urine running down my leg.
Welp. So much for fixing it myself.

And just when I thought things couldn't get worse, the pee found
its way into my slippers. My brand-new slippers. At that moment, I
had two choices: I could be mad, or I could laugh. And since getting
mad wasn't going to magically dry off my feet, I laughed. Hard.

Still giggling, I hit the call button for the nurse, hoping she could
get here before things got even worse.

When she walked in, I greeted her with, "Sooo... funny story..."
She took one look at me, then at my soggy slippers, and sighed. But
in the best way. She checked the damage, gave me a knowing look,
and said, "Well, this could have been worse."

Oh, COULD it?!

Thankfully, she was right. A quick snap back together, a little
medical tape for reinforcement, and boom—good as new. Well, the
catheter was good as new. My dignity? That was still in critical
condition.

As she helped me clean up, we both just kept laughing—because
really, what else can you do? Otherwise, you're just a woman sitting
in a puddle of pee, and that's just sad.

-Deanna

Deanna's Final Threads

LOVE, LAUGHTER AND LEGACY

*D*uring Deanna's greatest decline, her Facebook posts offer a profound glimpse into her authentic and courageous journey. In sharing these heartfelt messages, we honor her unwavering honesty and the strength she displayed in her most challenging moments. Her words stand as a testament to her faith, resilience, and love, inspiring all who read them to embrace vulnerability, truth, and the power of living fully.

December 12, 2024:

Over this last week, my hospice nurse noted significant declines with my breathing and swallowing. It's times like this, when progression is very obvious and undeniable, that it hits all over again.

There are peaks and valleys with terminal disease!

When I got diagnosed with ALS at the end of January (2024), I immediately called a family meeting. Although I had already had individual conversations with my closest family, including my husband, children, sisters, parents, etc., the official diagnosis led to bringing everybody together to talk over what this really meant, and the seriousness of what was to come. ALS is a fatal neuromuscular disease. There is no cure, and there is no chance of surviving this disease.

This was a fact that was important to accept early on...

Next, talking about dying, what my wishes were through the dying stages, and discussing uncomfortable things about hopes and dreams for my family after I'm gone had to be normalized. I'm so thankful we have spent the last 10 months living our best lives together and discussing my end-of-life wishes even at the dinner table or over a board game like it was an everyday conversation... because, for our family, that's what it had to become.

Tonight the hospice team came over to meet with my family and talk with us all together about the care plan I desire. They answered questions regarding comfort medications, what the end-of-life dying stages are, and modifications we can consider to make me more comfortable and so much more.

Talking about dying, or losing our loved ones, can feel incredibly difficult or uncomfortable, but I can say it has been an honor and a blessing to be able to walk my family through this process with me, instead of without me.

P.S. ALS YOU SUCK, but you never stole our joy!

#ALS #ALSawareness #ALSsucks #Hospice #care #dyingforacure #prayerworks #prayers #Godisgood #forever #peace #planner #seeyouthere #memories #memoriestokeep

December 17, 2024:

"Trust in the Lord with all your heart and lean not on your own understanding, in all your ways acknowledge Him and He will make your paths straight." Proverbs 3:5-6

This wisdom has been the instruction above all instructions for my life as a Christ follower. (This is my life verse).

"I make my plans and He directs my steps." Proverbs 16:9

I've always needed the 3-6 month plan... so wisdom says make the plan. I learned true wisdom was in taking action and planning to be the hands and feet of Jesus every day...

A life that produces spiritual maturity bears its fruit when we surrender to His steps that lead to outcomes that can only glorify God in the end.

All of this... Even now...

December 17, 2024:

Caregiving is not for the faint of heart.

The last couple of days have not only been extra difficult on me, but my caregivers feel the burdens as well.

Oren Cotten has been up the last couple of nights trying to figure out how to help me and get me comfortable. He has not gotten much sleep at all.

I had to text Dianna Wiebe at 5 a.m. this morning to come over as soon as possible. She always shows up, but I had to ask for the moon and stars to get through this one. I don't think I've been this sick ever. Pneumonia is awful...

Lots of changes in general. I haven't eaten since Friday, but I am still getting in about 40 oz of fluids. Oxygen levels are on a bit of a roller-coaster ride, and I downright don't feel good at all.

Thank you to my husband and best friend for accommodating day in and day out. This is not the chapter we wrote, but I appreciate the next-level care and support.

Deanna and Kory with matching Tattoos

December 20, 2024:

Wisdom worth leaving behind.
Some may look at my life and conclude I took the scenic route, or more difficult route of life lol. It's true! My shenanigans and pursuit of wisdom has often cost me a great deal of time, money, and resources.
I believe none of it goes to waste, but is used to further the kingdom of God by allowing my life journey to become someone else's survival guide.

Earlier this week someone asked me what does it mean to pursue wisdom? What does this look like in real life as we walk with God? knew what I believed about wisdom, but this question challenged me to really process what it takes to grow in knowledge and understanding, ultimately attaining wisdom.

Wisdom is granted by God when we seek it. It's attainable when we open our hearts and minds to new experiences, opportunities, and relationships that don't always promise a specific outcome. I've always tried to put myself in other people's shoes and seek to understand life from their perspective and worldview. Being open-minded has allowed me to have more control over my decisions, which also allows me to keep my own emotions in check without compromising my own morals, values, and beliefs. (This has been a work in progress for many years, and will continue to be.)

- Wisdom is often gained through making mistakes. Which can make it difficult to purposefully seek wisdom. I never wanted to be afraid to make mistakes. I've been known to jump off the cliff before spreading my wings... and I've also been known to spread my wings and jump without knowing where I would land. Every time I jumped, there were opportunities to learn, grow, and persevere. Some more difficult, tragic, life-changing, or hard. Regardless... no experience escaped me without it being transformational.

- Ask questions and spend time finding answers from multiple perspectives! I always thought there were two sides to every story, but over the years I learned, there are 3: YOURS, MINE, and HIS.

- The more curious you become, the more opportunities and experiences you open yourself up to, helping you make future decisions and build AMAZING relationships. It is possible to set the example in life and love and show compassion (even if they have differing beliefs or ideas), empathy (even if it seems undeserving), and understanding (because there may be more to the story). Blessed are those who find wisdom, those who gain understanding, for she is more profitable than silver and yields better returns than gold. - Proverbs 3:13-14

December 20, 2024:

This week has been a bit of a blur.
As time gets shorter, the world around me keeps its pace. There's a mixture of emotions... it's comforting to know everyone can and will be okay when I'm gone. It's difficult to know that I'm not needed for much anymore. It's peaceful knowing everyone is in good hands, which is why they don't need me. But this in-between can be lonely... nurses come, caregivers care, friends and family visit... but time spent with me now is squeezed into their everyday lives filled with the world that still goes on for them.

There is beauty in knowing you are not replaceable because there is only one you... but that your loved ones can and will keep moving without you. It's also hard to be present enough to see everyone keep going without you but disconnected enough to not know (or be able to track) what is happening this side of heaven.

Watching the world keep moving without you while you are still here is a strange phenomenon. I can't quite explain it or fully understand it, but it's painfully and peacefully felt.

P.S. ALS YOU SUCK
#lifegoeson #hospicecare #prayers #Godisgood #hospice #peaceful #comfort

December 24, 2024:

Shout out to these AMAZING kids I get to call mine!
I was in no shape to pull together my Christmas Eve traditions this year. I

decided I would give them all cash and call it good. I really was just looking forward to spending time with everyone.

My Amazing Children

Not only did Ashley Cotten and Reona Deleon pull together my tradition of Christmas Eve pajama boxes, but Leah Cotten couldn't let it slide without our annual stockings filled with each kid's favorite junk foods.

Kevin Cotten, Laura Cotten, and Jordan Kopas made sure the tree was filled. My mom Lynnea Cook wrapped a few last-minute gifts I forgot about and made dinner.

It feels so good to see my kids pull this together this year! Thank you, everyone, for keeping my traditions alive this year. My heart is so full, and I'm so thankful for you all.

December 25, 2024:

On December 23, Leah Cotten asked me if we were getting stockings this year. I responded with, "No, I haven't been able to pull any of that together, so it'll just be what it is."

Our "junk food" stockings are a tradition that holds significant meaning. They take me back to a time of difficulty in our family. But I've never told my kids the story of where this tradition came from... until tonight.

Stockings are Stuffed - Christmas 2024

My husband, Oren Cotten, almost died from MRSA pneumonia in 2012, resulting in a sudden relocation to CO to receive extensive treatment. His recovery time was 13 months before he was released to return to work. It would then take nearly 4 months to get hired on at a department. He was our sole provider, with 4 kids under the ages of 8. We stretched a fairly small savings ($30,000) over the next 17 months.

Times were very difficult, but not impossible. We had no money for gifts that year, so I had to get creative. We bought one family gift (a Wii gaming system), and I used our food stamps to fill their stockings with some of their favorite treats.

Since then, it has become a yearly tradition to fill their stockings with junk foods they love.

On Christmas Eve, Leah asked me for my debit card and made her way out to shop. She filled the stockings! She had no idea how much it meant to me to see this tradition continue this year.

#christmas2024 #Christmas #comfort #memories #family #stockingstuffers #traditions #Godisgoodallthetime #Godisgood

December 25, 2024:

I had 4 kids in 5 years. Limiting chaos while my kids were little was a mission I spent years trying to master lol.

Christmas has a way of creating excitement in littles that is difficult to contain, especially for tired moms with a handful of toddlers and babies. Getting the kids to go to bed so Santa can come was extra chaotic. After Laura was born, I came up with a plan to get my kids to go to bed at a decent hour on Christmas Eve.

Christmas Eve boxes - filled with their brand-new Christmas jammies, hot cocoa packets, and popcorn. Topped off with a family gift, the new movie of the year in DVD format.

I would make a pot of chili, watch a family movie, and everyone was excited to get into their Christmas jammies.

The secret to those jammies? It was Santa's cue to come to our house. If they weren't asleep when he arrived, Santa would have to skip our house, and it would be difficult to get him to turn around.

Pajama Party Christmas 2024

As they got older (and DVDs became a thing of the past), we started going to the theater... and after the shutdown in 2020, we started streaming our movie at home.

Christmas Eve PJs - Cotten family Christmas tradition made possible this year by Ashley Cotten and Reona Deleon! They added a little twist with Christmas socks and a new game, *Hues and Cues*!

Christmas Eve 2024 was spent with family and was such a blessed time of food, gifts, eggnog lattes, games, laughter, and a few tears.

#Christmas #christmas2024 #memories #family #Godisgood #traditions #blessed #blessedbeyondmeasure #pajamaparty

December 29, 2024:

2024 Year in Review Part 1 (January - May)

Although I had set goals I had hoped to achieve in 2024 (but I can't remember what they were haha), my plans quickly changed when I walked into 2024 with a terminal diagnosis.

2024 was all about spending time with my loved ones, making memories, and living life to the fullest. It was also a year of many firsts and many lasts. But... I couldn't be more blessed looking back at so many incredible moments with friends and family.

2025 looks a little different, and that's okay! It's one day at a time right now, and I cherish every memory behind me and look forward to all the goodness in front of me.

#2024recap #newyear #LookingAhead #LookingForwardTo2025 #lookingback #makingmemories2024 #blessed #family #friends #opportunities #familyfun #thankful #HappyNewYear

December 29, 2024:

2024 Year in Review Part 2 (June - December)

Although I had set goals I had hoped to achieve in 2024 (but I can't remember what they were haha), my plans quickly changed when I walked into 2024 with a terminal diagnosis.

2024 was all about spending time with my loved ones, making memories, and living life to the fullest. It was also a year of many firsts and many lasts. But... I couldn't be more blessed looking back at so many incredible moments with friends and family.

2025 looks a little different, and that's okay! It's one day at a time right now, and I cherish every memory behind me and look forward to all the goodness in front of me.

#2024recap #newyear #LookingAhead #LookingForwardTo2025 #lookingback #makingmemories2024 #blessed #family #friends #opportunities #familyfun #thankful #HappyNewYear

December 30, 2024:

I'll never forget my first home health nurse, Karla, saying to me, "Girl, you still got one good Christmas in you."

It gave me something to look forward to!

There were times it felt impossible, but it's safe to say I made it... and it hasn't been easy.

Around Thanksgiving, I noticed things really changing. Of course, ALS is progressive in nature, so I'm always declining per se, but I was struggling to do the things I normally would do like therapies (PT/Speech), venture out for shopping or lunch, coffee dates, etc. My appetite decreased greatly, and I was sleeping a lot more, like 15+ hours a day.

When I had to miss my hair appointment this month, that was the eye-opener... I don't miss hair appointments, as you all know.

Aspiration pneumonia tried to take me out, and no promises it won't because I'm still fighting that battle, but I remain hopeful! I started another round of antibiotics today, and this week we're getting cough assist on board. Some other little things we're doing to help conserve my energy are having hospice bring a hospital bed with rails to make it easier to get in and out of bed.

I don't know what 2025 looks like, but I know I'm blessed I made it this far.

P.S. ALS YOU SUCK, but I'm still winning.

#ALS #ALSawareness #ALSsucks #hospice #2024to2025 #today #still #bestill #hope #God #Godisgood #HopeAndHealing #blessed

January 1, 2025:

I am a MASTER STRATEGIC PLANNER!

Like every other year, I had 2024 all planned with SMART goals aligned. I came into 2024 like a wrecking ball, at full speed ahead, like N.O.T.H.I .N.G could get in my way this year.
We can make our plans, but the LORD determines our steps. ~Proverbs 16:9
And then... 2024.
It looked like this:

- Diagnosed with a terminal disease (ALS)... not a box I planned to check.

- Family trip to the Bahamas as prescribed by Dr. Ker.

- Closed my business coaching and consulting business.

- Fulfilled Oren's Christmas 2023 gift! A trip to Punta Cana that I scored for $582.

- I attended my first family reunion on my mom's side in San Antonio, TX.

- I started my arm sleeve that tells a whole story of God's healing and redemption.

- Visited "The End" - one of 4 working lighthouses left in Montauk, NY.

- I finished my largest diamond art project (27x37in canvas) with

105,000 diamonds and 62 colors with struggling fine motor skills.

- Sold that diamond art piece for $5,000 at the Casper Christian Schools annual fundraiser.

- Outlined a book, *"Embracing the End"* (I tried to skip this, but coming soon by popular demand, stay tuned).

- Binged season 6 of *Virgin* (IYKYK)... I definitely need to live long enough to see season 7.

- Celebrated chapter 43.

2024 also came with really tough goodbyes. My father-in-law gained his angel wings on March 31, and my niece, Alli, was welcomed home on December 6.

2024... there was so much more. I checked a lot of boxes, but these memories and experiences were not reserved in the 2024 strategic plan (except Punta Cana, of course). It's fair to say that 2024 was lived out with more purpose and intention than the strategic plan accounted for.

I'm coming into 2025 slow and steady and without a strategic plan. This season is different... no goals, no agenda, nothing planned... and I don't even feel lost... But... I am ready to embrace each minute, hour, and day. I will continue to serve the Lord and show up as long as I have breath in my lungs.

Hey there, January 1, 2025! What are we doing today?

#HappyNewYear #goodbye2024 #stillfighting #ALS #ALSawareness #hospice #HopeAndHealing #hope #blessed #thankful #God #Godisgood

January 2, 2025:

This month's hair is titled "Sunset," and it's AMAZING! There is so much reason and purpose in this month's design.

The sunrise and the sunset remind me of God's promises. He is the maker of the sun, and every day the sun rises urging me to wake up because He has given me breath in my lungs. That means I have the strength to make it through this day. As the sun sets, it reminds me that I am safe in His arms, I can be calm and rest. As He consistently rises and sets the sun, how much more can I trust He will follow through on the promises of His word.

Thank you, Kori Hoersten, for not only hearing my heart but using it to inspire unique hair designs. You have come up with something so rad every time.

And an even bigger thank you for recognizing when I could no longer get to you at the salon and going straight into action, ordering this cool contraption to use at my kitchen sink. I would have never expected you to come to my home, but I'm forever grateful.

Always take care of your hair!

You make my heart smile! You have gone above and beyond encouraging me to keep up on my hair this year because you always see it bring me life. It has meant the world to me to not only feel great but to have this time with you. Thank you for stepping up and coordinating end-of-life details on my behalf. Thank you for checking in all the time and for just coming to sit with me when I need company. ... and this memory... our matching tattoos! It's a great way to constantly remind us that there is never a bad time to go to the beach.

You will forever be the best hairstylist, but even more my dear sister and friend.

For those needing accessible options for washing hair in the kitchen sink, this was so easy to use and never made a mess. I'd definitely give this a 5-star for those of you needing to do your hair at home and from the comfort of your wheelchair.

January 7, 2025:

"Because of the LORD's great love, we are not consumed, for his compassions never fail. They are new every morning; great is your faithfulness." Lamentations 3:22-23

I've always said if God wanted me to see the sunrise, He would have scheduled it for 8 AM! As beautiful as the sunrise is, I'd much rather sleep in and enjoy the view from heaven someday.

But lately... my sleep schedule is a mess! Some days I'm sleeping for 15+ hours a day. I have never known a time I can sleep all night and not wake up until it's getting dark again, but that's so real right now. Other days I'm awake for 20+ hours a day, waking up at 10 AM, and staying awake all day and all night.

Yesterday I got to meet my newborn niece. My sister said something I feel like I know, but when she said it, I felt it. Knowing and feeling something are profoundly different. When you feel something, it's more than being able to define it, it comes with empathy and compassion.

She's up all night right now too... and she reminded me, "this is only a season."

Feeling that one in my bones!

Whatever this day has in store, I'm here for it... I might not be awake or coherent, but I'm here.

Thankful for another day!

#thankful #grateful #blessed

January 9, 2025:

I am the patient... my husband just tucked me into my hospital bed. As I'm laying here, having a coughing fit that burns my lungs, it's hard not to remember what once was. It's hard to know that I'll never go back to what once was (unless God has a miracle that I'm not aware of yet). Although I'm confident the view from Heaven is way better.

What I can do is look back and know I'm thankful that I was always that person that "did it scared." Most days I "did it tired..."

Gift from Facebook friend Michael Humel

I'm sad and I'm mad, but I'm also so thankful I received answers and got to enjoy this last year purposefully making memories, even when I "wasn't motivated!"

Don't waste a moment! I recall booking our cruise last year (6 weeks after my diagnosis), and I asked myself, "Am I booking this too soon?" I had to ask myself, "Will you ever regret this time?" The answer was no, and now that I can't travel, I'm grateful I didn't let fear and denial creep in and guide me.

If you aren't sure if you should, maybe you can't see how you will be able to take the time off, maybe you aren't sure your job will give you the time, maybe you're not sure how you'll pay for it... whatever the reason, ask yourself, "But if I DO (even despite the unknown) will I ever regret this decision?"

If the answer is NO, make it happen! One day, it could be you, in that hospital bed, regretting all the things you wish you would have done scared, tired, alone, and unmotivated!

January 11, 2025:

Real friends don't care if you're dying...

You party poop and they are playin' the pranks. Thankful for amazing friends that always remember I haven't lost my sense of humor...

I laughed so hard waking up to this...

January 12, 2025:

One year ago today, I called my spine doctor's office to cancel a Botox injection in my thoracic region. I explained to the office that I had experienced some pro-

Never lose your sense of humor

gression since my last appointment with him, so at this point, my PCP recommended we hold off on this procedure and potentially run the risk of covering anything up, making it more difficult to get to a diagnosis.

The girl that took the call told me that she would pass on the message, and of course, I apologized for calling two hours before my appointment to cancel.

Shortly after we hung up, I received a call back from the nurse, asking if I would still be willing to come in so that my spine doctor could take a look at the progression I had experienced since my last appointments with him. Of course, I agreed to do that, and they were happy to cancel the procedural part of that appointment.

My spine doctor spent a little over an hour completing one of the most thorough exams I had had up to this point.

And then he asked me, "Do you want me to shoot straight with you?"

And I said absolutely! At this point, I was really struggling with one of my hands, one of my legs, and holding up my posture and needing to sleep sitting up. I'm a "let's get things done so I can move forward" kind of person. After suffering from multiple autoimmune diseases over the years, I felt this would just add another treatable, but annoying, diagnosis. I could just take another pill, change my diet a little, maybe look at my sleep schedule again, etc. Up to this point, I believed everything was treatable.

I could not have been prepared for what he was about to tell me!

He said, "I am 95% sure this is ALS."

I had not yet had a four-quadrant EMG, and that is the most diagnostic tool available to diagnose ALS after mimicking diseases have been ruled out.

I walked out of the office that day; it was freezing cold, and I sat in my car, just numb.

But, that 5%? I held onto that so tightly.

Just a short two weeks later, I went in for a four-quadrant EMG. I had fibrillations and fasciculations in three out of four quadrants. I left there with my results in hand, with a diagnosis of "Definite ALS."

#ALS #ALSawareness #ALSsucks #fighter #onedayatatime #prayers #terminal #dyingforacure #Godisgood #Godisgoodallthetime #healthjourney

January 16, 2025:

Last night we had an appointment at the funeral home. It was just me, my husband Oren Cotten, and our very dear friend, Kori Hoersten, also known as my rad hairstylist and funeral/celebration of life planner. She's a jack of all trades, seriously!

It feels a little strange to get to be an active player in all of this planning. Denial creeps in and makes one wonder, "But what if I don't die? Why did I take all of these steps if I didn't actually need to?"

Then I remember 100% of us are making an exit from this life. It's never too early to plan for your impending death. Planning and putting as much of your final wishes into place relieves so much pressure on your family in the end.

It did feel good to get this appointment taken care of and know decisions are made.

In other news! I finished my second round of antibiotics for the aspiration pneumonia a little over a week ago. I know that there is no promise or guarantee with the antibiotics that I took, but they did bring some level of comfort as far as symptoms go.

But this last week has reminded me that the fight is HARD, but it's not over yet! I'm currently still battling all the gunk in my lungs, as well as a UTI and now a nasty head cold. I don't know if it's turning into a sinus infection or what!

Got a call into the doctor to find out, but in the meantime, I'm still here, and I'm still kicking.

THANK YOU for the constant showers of prayers, love, and support.

February 2, 2025

It's been a wild two weeks. The hardest part is realizing it's been two weeks since my admission at Hospice... and also trying to wrap my head around the fact that I was sedated long enough to make me literally ask every day, "What is today?" ... A few days ago, I learned from my husband there was a point they weren't sure I would make it. I'm glad they waited a few days after I woke up to tell me that. It was a level of processing that was greatly needed. Definitely making a turnaround, it does seem the medication regimen is working to keep me comfortable.

I did have to set some boundaries with visitors to make sure I complete some workloads (only I would be in Hospice still thinking about work, but #iykyk) ... I've got some boxes that need to be checked and need to make sure I accom-

Me with my niece and nephews modate proper rest times. Thank you all for hanging with me as I had a little breakdown that helped me get some boundaries in place and keep things moving forward.

I have a decent view from my room, the bed is comfortable, I have what I need, and the icing on the cake... feeling like my head is cleared a bit more. It's important I take advantage of these days in front of me to complete some work-related tasks and legacy items I hold near and dear.

Precious 'face' making pic with me and my nephew

It's a brand new week in front of me! Thank you for praying for me and getting me to this point.

P.S. Note the confusion in my face a week ago and the clarity and comical moment I got with my nephew. Speaks volumes! I know it's not a cure, but it's the open window of time to pick up some pieces, and I'm thankful.

March 6, 2025

The Separation of Time

When I was first diagnosed, everything around me took on a new or heightened sense of appreciation. The people I loved. The trees. The flowers. The blue sky. My strengths and talents. A deep thankfulness and gratitude filled me—an awareness of the beauty and privilege of living on this side of heaven.

Then, in July, I noticed a shift. The same things that once stirred thankfulness in me began to change in meaning. I started to see everything differently—not with more appreciation, but with the realization that even the most beautiful things here could never compare to what awaits in heaven.

I didn't feel like I was *dying*, but I could feel the world around me beginning to fade in importance. The things that once held so much weight, the things I once clung to, no longer seemed as significant. Three weeks later, my doctor confirmed what my heart already knew. If my respiratory function continued to decline at the same rate and I refused life-extending measures, he would recommend hospice. He explained that hospice wasn't just for the actively dying, as many assume, but rather a means to ensure a higher quality of care as we near the end of life.

"And if I go and prepare a place for you, I will come back and take you to be with me that you also may be where I am." —John 14:3

I began my home hospice journey in mid-November 2024. Then, on January 17, 2025, I was admitted to my local hospice hospital. The days passed, though I barely noticed them. I wasn't living by a clock anymore—just being present, just being still.

On March 6, my parents and my husband came to visit, bringing games to play. In the middle of our conversation, Oren mentioned something about March, and I instinctively responded, "Wait, what? Why did you say March?" I looked down at my phone—and sure enough, it was March 6.

I sat there, stunned.

How had time slipped by so quickly?

In that moment, I realized just how much time separates us from heaven and earth. Here, on earth, time moves, shifts, and slips through our fingers. But in heaven, there is no time. No waiting. No delay.

"And he swore by him who lives forever and ever, who created the heavens and all that is in them, the earth and all that is in it, and the sea and all that is in it, and said, 'There will be no more delay!'" —Revelation 10:6

I thought back to the days when time seemed to stretch endlessly before me. When years felt long, when I worried about what was next, when I tried to control what was coming. But now, I saw time differently. It was only a thin veil, separating me from eternity.

I am not afraid.

I know what awaits.

And when that moment comes—when the last second of time fades and I step into eternity—there will be no more sorrow, no more pain, no more tears.

"He will wipe every tear from their eyes. There will be no more death or mourning or crying or pain, for the old order of things has passed away." —Revelation 21:4

Time moves fast here. But where I'm going... time doesn't exist at all.

One More Time, Capturing Love

*D*uring **Deanna's greatest decline**, she remained committed to what mattered most—**love, family, and making memories.** Even in hospice, she embraced the beauty of each fleeting moment, ensuring that those she cherished had something to hold onto long after she was gone. These final family photos are not about saying goodbye, but about **celebrating the love, laughter, and connection that defined her life.** They are a reflection of her unwavering spirit—proof that even in the hardest moments, love remains.

*Deanna, her husband, her chil-
dren and their loves*

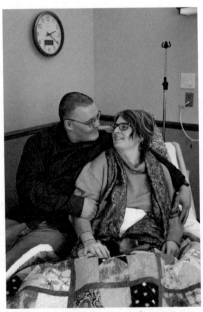

Deanna and her true love, Oren

Deanna's Mom and Dad

Deanna with her family and In-laws

Deanna and her oldest

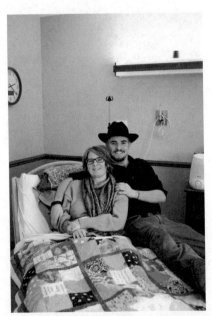

Deanna and her son

Deanna with her third born

Deanna with her youngest

Deanna with her biological Dad

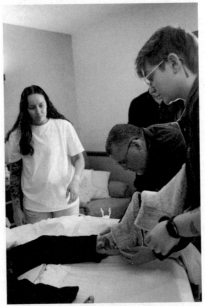

*The family helping Deanna get
ready for pictures*

*Deanna's family helping her out
of bed .*

Deanna and her family

Deanna with her best friends

Deanna and her daughters

Deanna and her daughters girl-friend

The Story Behind Dammit Dede

In 2015, we were living in Colorado, and we'd often visit my husband's grandfather's land up on Black Mesa. It was our little escape, where nature provided everything—fresh spring water, wild raspberries, and a whole lot of memories. Every time we went, we'd take our five-gallon buckets, fill them with water from the natural springs, and pick raspberries by the handful, stuffing our hats full.

Oren always told me and the kids, *"Just pick along the pathline. There's plenty there. No need to go down the hills."*

Well, I don't always listen.

There was this one perfect little patch of berries just out of reach, and I figured if I put my foot on a tiny ledge, I could grab them. Big mistake. The moment my foot touched that ledge, it gave way, and I went **sliding**—twenty feet straight down the mountainside, bouncing off baby trees, rocks, and bushes, scraping myself up from head to toe.

And do you know the first thing out of Oren's mouth?

"Dammit, Dede."

Not *"Are you okay?"* Not *"Do you need help?"* Just **"Dammit, Dede."**

That was the day I realized something—I'd been blamed for everything for **years** and hadn't even noticed! Every time the kids got hurt, ran into something, needed stitches, or even stubbed a toe, Oren would say, *"Dammit, Dede."* Like somehow, through osmosis or sheer force of existence, it was always my fault. But until that moment—laying at the bottom of that mountain, scratched up like I lost a fight with a porcupine—I hadn't caught on.

Climbing back up that mountainside was no joke. When I finally made it back to camp, my mother-in-law pulled out her collection of old-school holistic remedies to patch me up. Nothing was broken, just a whole lot of soreness (and a bruised ego).

And from that day forward, it became a **thing.**

If someone got hurt? *"Dammit, Dede."*
If something went wrong? *"Dammit, Dede."*
Didn't matter if I was even **there**—it was my fault. LOL.

We didn't fully realize how funny it was until it was **my** turn to take the fall—literally. And honestly? I wouldn't have it any other way.

Dammit Dede

This page is a tribute to Deanna's incredible legacy—the laughter she shared, the strength she embodied, and the way she made life just a little bit brighter (and a whole lot funnier) for all of us.

If you're here, you probably have a 'Dammit, Dede' story of your own. Whether it was something she said, something she did, or just the way she made you feel like you could take on the world—Deanna had a way of leaving a mark. Maybe it was one of those moments when everything went sideways, and instead of panicking, she laughed (and made sure you did, too). Or maybe it was the way she lived—full of grit, grace, and just enough mischief to keep things interesting. Or maybe—let's be real—you just needed someone else to blame.

And from now on, you have full permission to say "Dammit, Dede" in your own life whenever something ridiculous happens—or when you just need a good excuse. Trust us, she'd love that. So go ahead, write those funny Dammit, Dede moments below and keep her spirit alive in the best way possible.

Take a moment to reflect on her journey. Fill in the dates to honor her time here, then write her a letter—share a memory, a lesson she taught you, or simply tell her how her courage, humor, and resilience continue to inspire you.

Deanna Cotten December 23, 1981 – _____

Dear Deanna,

"Your words honor her journey and keep her legacy alive."

Punta Cana 2024

Packing for myself has gotten trickier lately, but since I was heading out of the country, I made sure to handle it on my own. I packed my swimsuit—a trusty tankini top with shorts—because, let's be honest, I only shave the things that need to be shaved for swimming.

Apparently, my husband decided to go on a little shopping spree before my trip. Fast forward to Punta Cana—I go to grab my swimsuit and realize something's missing.

"Where are my blue swimsuit shorts?" I ask.

From the bathroom, he starts laughing—laughing—before casually admitting, "Oh, I didn't have room for those swimsuits, so I put them back."

OH NO HE DIDN'T.

He replaced my practical swimwear with five—yes, FIVE—thong bikinis. Let me tell you, I almost came back a widow. I was that pissed.

Now, here's where it gets worse. I have Hashimoto's, and let's just say I grow hair in places I don't want hair. Shaving where the sun doesn't shine? A nightmare. I have tried every cream, lotion, and trick to avoid razor burn, but my skin simply refuses to cooperate. Waxing? Forget it. The hair just laughs and stays put.

Day one was fine. But by day two? My entire backside was on fire. Red, irritated—every step felt like punishment. I had to put on a cover-up, and I made my husband get in the pool first before I dared to follow.

"Everyone here has one of these on," he said, trying to reassure me. "NOT EVERYONE HAS RAZOR BURN ALL OVER THEIR BUTT!"

Never again. Never. Again.

He made it back alive. We are living out our bucket list— apparently, his is different than mine. I still love him.
-Deanna

Available Soon – Slightly Used, Fully Housebroken

Ladies, listen up! This one right here—20 years of training, and he's finally ready for the world (you're welcome). You are about to get the best version of him. #iykyk

He's an amazing man, stuck with me through thick and thin, even death didn't scare him off—so if you've got a flair for drama, sorry, you'll have to up your game. He's already raised four kids (all still alive and functioning members of society), so no parenting required—just be a decent human to them, and when grandkids come, embrace your inner grandma (bonus points if you make killer cookies).

Now, a few survival tips:

- Keep him traveling—he loves it. However, be warned: he prefers living in a walk-in freezer, so drag him to a beach at least once a year to thaw yourself out.
- Encourage his hobbies—fishing, hunting, camping, shooting (yep, buy the man all the ammo, but maybe keep a lawyer on retainer).
- Game nights are a must—but don't expect him to schedule them. If left to his own devices, the only thing he'll schedule is... well, nothing. Including trips to see his mom in Colorado—PLEASE make sure he goes. She's important.

Most importantly, this man loves with his whole heart. He's a big ol' teddy bear who will wipe your tears, cuddle you when you need it, and remind you daily that you're loved.

And one last thing—help him remember: he's not replacing Dede. Instead, he is blessed with a second love story—one that I fully endorse, because God's got this. Now go on, apply within. Serious inquiries only.

-Deanna

Amazon, You Win (Again)

So remember when my watches got stolen? Yeah, that was a rough day. I swore off Amazon like a woman on a mission—declared my independence, took a stand, and told the world (or at least my Facebook friends) that I was DONE. No more one-click ordering, no more late-night impulse buys, no more cardboard boxes stacked to the ceiling like I was running an underground shipping operation.

And I held strong! I made it through the holidays Amazon-free, flexing my self-control like some kind of online shopping monk. Then... reality hit.

I needed an urn. And not just any urn—the perfect urn. Where did I find it? Oh, you already know where this is going. Amazon.

So, I swallowed my pride, posted the urn picture on Facebook, and announced to the world:

"Alright, Amazon. You get one more chance. But if this package gets stolen, I hope the thief needs it before I do." 😄😄😄

And y'all, the comments did not disappoint.

The best one—the one that sent me into an actual wheezing fit— was this gem:

"If they leave the empty box, you can just plan to go in that." 😆
😆😆

I have never laughed so hard in my life. At this point, I might just order a second one—just in case.

-Deanna

Deanna's Final Resting Place

About the Author

Deanna Cotten was a wife, mother, and woman of faith who inspired countless people with her courage, humor, and resilience. Diagnosed with ALS, Deanna embraced life's final chapter with unwavering grace and purpose, finding joy in the small moments and hope in her faith.

Deanna Cotten

Her journey, captured in *Embracing the End*, is a testament to her belief that love, laughter, and connection are the greatest legacies we can leave behind. Deanna's story continues to inspire others to live fully, love deeply, and face life's challenges with strength and gratitude.

What Can You Do?

Deanna's journey has touched countless hearts with her resilience, faith, and love for her family. Now, as we honor her incredible legacy, there are ways you can help carry her light forward and support the family she cherished so deeply.

Deanna, lovingly known as "Dede," leaves behind her devoted husband and four children—two teenagers and two young adults—who are navigating their grief while honoring her memory. Your support can make a profound difference in helping them through this difficult season.

Here's how you can help:

- Encourage your friends and family to purchase this book—every royalty goes directly to the family. Oren plans to divide the proceeds among all four children to help build their IRAs, securing their future.

- **Contribute to the Medical Fund:** We've set up a medical fund account to support Deanna's family. Checks can be sent to: **Converse County Bank**

P.O. Box 689

Douglas, WY 82633

Please make checks payable to **"Deanna Cotten Medical."**

For inquiries, you can call Converse County Bank at **307-358-5300.**

- **Support Deanna's Family** As we honor Deanna's incredible life and legacy, we have the opportunity to come together and support the ones she loved most—her family. Oren and their four children meant everything to her, and now we can give back in a meaningful way. Please consider making a donation to help provide for Deanna's family during this time. Every contribution, no matter the size, makes a difference.

 **Click the link to donate:** GiveSendGo – Support Deanna's Family Thank you for your kindness, love, and generosity. Please share this with others who may want to help. #SupportDeannasFamily #ALS #LoveInAction

- **Shop Dede-Strong Merchandise:** Visit https://dede-strong.printify.me/ to purchase inspiring merch that carries Deanna's spirit of strength, humor, and resilience. Every purchase helps support her family while spreading her powerful message to others.

Scan to access Dede Strong Merch Store

- **Leave a Verified Amazon Review:** If Deanna's story has impacted you, share your thoughts in a verified review on Amazon. Reviews help the book reach more readers who can benefit from her story of hope and purpose. Your words have the power to inspire someone to pick up *Embracing the End* and find the courage to face their own journey.

- **Spread the Word:** Tell others about *Embracing the End*. Share it on social media, gift it to friends and loved ones, or mention it in your community. Deanna's message of love, faith, and living intentionally deserves to be shared far and wide.

Your Impact Matters

By supporting Dede's family, you are helping them heal and carry forward the lessons she taught them—lessons of grace, resilience, and living fully in the face of life's challenges. Together, we can honor Deanna's legacy by ensuring her love and light continue to shine brightly in the lives of others.

Thank you for standing with us and keeping Deanna's story alive.

Are You Ready

TO TURN YOUR TESTIMONY INTO A PUBLISHED LEGACY—LIKE DEANNA?

You've conquered your challenges—now it's time to turn your victory into a book that inspires the world!

At In The Zone, we help purpose-driven individuals transform their journey into a powerful, published book. From idea to impact, we walk with you every step of the way—guiding you through writing, editing, formatting, and publishing. Your story matters, and we're here to help you share it with confidence and excellence!

As Deanna says, *"Do not wait!"* **Your story matters.** It's time to get it out there.

Visit www.inthezone.live to start your author journey and join our exclusive author programs today!

Scan to check out the In The Zone website

Wendy and Deanna during the week Wendy and her husband flew in to surprise Deanna with a visit

Made in the USA
Columbia, SC
18 March 2025

55306612R00102